JOHN IRELAND
THE MAN AND HIS
MUSIC

BY MURIEL V. SEARLE

MIDAS BOOKS

By the same author for Midas:

Spas and Watering Places
Bathing Machines and Bloomers

First published in 1979 by
Midas Books, 12 Dene Way, Speldhurst,
Tunbridge Wells, Kent TN3 0NX

ISBN 0 85936 190 X (UK Cased)

Printed in Great Britain by Offset Lithography by
The Pitman Press, Bath.

Dedicated

to my father, *Noel Searle,* who met his future wife, my mother, through music.

M.V.S.

Acknowledgements

Without the help of three people in particular this book could never have been written.

Firstly, Mrs. Norah Kirby, a companion and confidante of Ireland's latter years; to her personal memories, records of the composer's youth and young manhood, and exacting checking of the manuscript the author owes an immense debt.

Secondly, Mr. Charles (Stafford) Markes; talking with him gave the author a deeper understanding of Ireland's music, and of the letters Mr. Markes kindly loaned.

Thirdly, Mrs. Marjorie Walde, in whose home Ireland stayed through most of the Second World War; without her store of memories and anecdotes, generously passed on, the writer's ability to convey something of Ireland's humour and humanity would have been greatly diminished.

Grateful thanks are also extended to many others who have lent letters and photographs, or related additional memories of Ireland as man and musician. They include:

Sir Thomas Armstrong
Mr. L. Bacon
Lady Barbirolli (Evelyn
    Rothwell)
Mrs. G. M. Beckett
Mr. A. Chappelow
Miss Ruth Dyson
Mr. Peter Racine Fricker
Mr. David H. Jones
Mr. John Longmire

Mr. T. J. Marsh
Mr. P. I. Middleton (British
    Music Society)
Mr. Bernard Naylor
Mr. Alan Rowlands
Mr. Stuart Scott
Mr. Brian Thomas
Mrs. Mary Turnbull
Mr. R. Vandyke

Foreword

All musicians will welcome a new book about John Ireland, one of the most interesting and complex characters among all our recent composers, whose whole output, all of it of great importance, yet fills a comparatively small space in any catalogue.

More surprising still, it includes no symphony, no opera, no string quartet, though he did write some quartets when a student.

Miss Searle is exceptionally well placed to undertake this study, and will be able to bring several points of view to the notice of her readers which will I hope help to arouse fresh interest in this fine music, particularly as most of it is now available on the records of the Lyrita Company, and so can be really well studied.

I was always pleased when an Ireland work found its way on to a programme I was to perform, and we were good friends.

ADRIAN C. BOULT

Miss Muriel Searle was commissioned to write this book by friends of John Ireland, and Midas Books were asked to be associated with its planning and production, also to reproduce the work as approved by John Ireland's executors in its original form.

Contents

1. John Ireland Through a Window

When the Great Fire of 1666 finally died down, after blazing fiercely for four days, the City of London as its inhabitants had known it all their lives no longer existed.

Four hundred streets had disappeared. Over thirteen thousand homes, from hovels to mansions of the mighty, were reduced to charred beams and warm cinders. Numerous public and company halls were destroyed, and business had ceased. A vast expanse of smouldering wreckage marked where England's capital had pulsed with human and commercial activity, barely a week ago. Old St. Paul's, the City's architectural centrepiece, was a gaunt, roofless, burned-out shell, still intermittently crackling as pockets of flame sparked afresh from heaps of grotesquely twisted debris. Nearly ninety other churches shared St. Pauls' fate.

Among the comparatively few ecclesiastical survivors of this historic holocaust was the ancient Church of the Holy Sepulchre, on the City's fringe, just far enough away to escape. This is therefore one of present-day London's oldest churches, from which the Crusaders set out to save the Holy Sepulchre itself from the Saracens. Its setting is not particularly attractive, hemmed in by the massive Old Bailey — centre of justice, and occupant of the site of notorious Newgate gaol — functional modern offices and shops, and Holborn Viaduct station. Behind the church are St. Bartholomew's Hospital and Smithfield meat market, contributing to London's daily din with wails of ambulance sirens and roars of refrigerated meat lorries from all over Europe. On all sides continuous traffic and crowds of harrassed-looking people add to the cacophonous uproar of a great city, which ceases only late at night or on Sundays. Noise is a normal part of existence for the thousands who travel up daily to work in this part of London.

Yet, in the midst of the crowds and hubbub, there is always a refuge, standing aloof and representing the complete antithesis of unmelodious, inharmonious noise; this church which has become synonymous with sounds that relax, soothe and uplift the tired mind—sounds of music.

The Church of the Holy Sepulchre (colloquially but incorrectly known as St. Sepulchre's) is the Musicians' Church of London. Here composers and performers of national stature, together with many who gave their lives to music-making on a more localised scale, are commemorated in monuments, windows, hassocks and furnishings. All year round the church is used for concerts, recitals, choral services, and special events commemorating landmarks in the musical calendar.

As far back as the 18th century famous musicians began to be associated with the church, when Handel is said to have played its fine Renatus Harris organ. Mendelssohn, too, reputedly touched this instrument's keys. Certainly Samuel Wesley and his musician son, also named Samuel, knew it. As a schoolboy Henry Wood took lessons here, and became assistant organist when he was only fourteen years old. Greatness usually reveals itself early.

When Sir Henry Wood, founder-conductor of the famous Henry Wood Promenade Concerts or Proms, died in 1944, his ashes were brought here, to rest in a wall niche under the central window, which is now dominated by St. Cecilia, patron saint of music, with her organ and angel trumpeters. Two lower stained glass panels portray Sir Henry as a boy organist of this church, and conducting a Prom at Queen's Hall.

Around Sir Henry Wood's window and memorial a chapel for musicians has developed. Almost every piece of furniture and embroidery was donated in a musician's memory. Each chair bears a memorial plaque. Every embroidered blue hassock incorporates a musician's name, dates, and a beautifully worked extract from one of his own works, or one associated with him. They span the entire field of music: composers (Parry, Elgar, Sir George Dyson); conductors (Sir Malcolm Sargent, Sir Eugene Goossens, Ernest Read); instrumentalists

2

(Dennis Brain, Harriet Cohen, Dame Myra Hess, W H Reed); and singers, such as Kathleen Ferrier. Other well-known figures remembered in this manner include Sir Sydney Nicholson, founder of the Royal School of Church Music. The blue sanctuary carpeting and a green Trinity altar frontal for the church itself are memorials to Sir Malcolm Sargent.

Above the Musicians' Chapel altar is a lovely *Magnificat* window to Walter Carroll, who did much to make children aware of music. Another large window shows Melba in two of her operatic roles, including Mimi in *La Boheme*. The Royal Opera House, Covent Garden, and the Royal Albert Hall, scenes of her greatest triumphs, are readily recognisable, together with the arms of her native Australia, Australian singing birds, and the Peach Melba ice-cream dish which will be perpetually associated with her.

A book of remembrance is regularly turned, page by page, each time revealing a new list of departed singers, players, composers and musical writers, many of whom were almost household names.

As the visitor to this Musicians' Chapel looks up from the page, he sees another majestic window, immediately above him, occupying most of the west wall. One name is inscribed there, on stained glass instead of parchment: John Ireland, 1879—1962, D Mus. Durham, Fellow RCM.

Six pictorial panels represent aspects of Ireland's life and work, or places which influenced the music of this great 20th century composer. Quotations in notation are interwoven. Some are immediately identifiable by Ireland devotees; others are more nebulous, suggesting rather than actually stating, in the manner of Ireland's more programmatic musical pictures.

The Musicians' Chapel epitomises peace, when approached out of London's discordant uproar. Yet the Ireland window is not so palely insipid as to avoid all suggestion of conflict— and neither was Ireland's music. Battles separated by some three thousand years are implied in two pictures. The savagery of warring primitive man inspired possibly the best of all his orchestral works, *Mai—Dun*, whose Dorset setting appears high above Ireland's head; and a Channel Islands scene reminds us that, from those islands which he so loved, Ireland

3

was among the last to escape, possessing nothing more than the unfinished score of *Sarnia*, ahead of the invading Nazis. But peace returns, in the winding Thames, Rock Mill, his Sussex home, doves of harmony, and reminders that the composer was a supreme country lover.

Even film music is represented; purists question the quality of this medium, often rightly; but Ireland was not alone among serious composers in producing film scores that were landmarks in their own right. Steers of the Australian plains therefore share this window with *The Holy Boy*, representing his music for the film classic, *The Overlanders*.

Wandering with the eye from section to section of John Ireland's window, we see more than symbols of the composer's best known works. Man and music being inseparable, we find also a human being who, throughout life, loved cats as much as crotchets, and whose humour was sharp without malice. And through the man, the music spontaneously wells up and out, not as a formal separate study but an extension of his mind and character. As the French, translated, say, 'Style is the man himself'.

Let us, therefore, enter the Musicians' Chapel, off the church's north aisle, forgetting that London lies outside. After looking at some of the fascinating memorial hassocks and reading the musical quotations upon them, in acknowledgement that music has always been kept alive by a vast army of people, each playing his part in the orchestra of human life, and never vested in just one personality, we will by instinct look upwards to the stained glass windows of Henry Wood, Melba, Walter Carroll and John Ireland.

For the purpose of this book, it is upon Ireland's window that we shall concentrate, chapter by chapter, for within this biography in glass lie clues to his symphony of life, from introduction to allegro, slow movement to finale and coda. Somewhere will be found a picture that corresponds to that symphony's first few bars, like a composer's traditional announcement of all that is to come; something representative of his formative years and early manhood.

2. To The Choristers of St. Luke's, Chelsea

At the foot of the John Ireland memorial window is a head-and-shoulders portrait of the composer himself, which captures something of the grave repose of his mellow mature years. He faces a panel in the greyish-blue glazing used for all six scenes depicting musical or topographical landmarks in his life, showing St. Luke's church, Chelsea, with the River Thames winding placidly in curves behind it.

St. Luke's marks the dividing line between his youth and professional musical career, and was the setting of Ireland's fully-fledged arrival as an organist.

Chelsea ran thereafter like a steadying continuo part, underlying the aforementioned symphony of life. Through most of the first half of the twentieth century, Chelsea was to be John Ireland's chief home town.

In attempting to understand Ireland as man and musician — why quality rather than quantity was always his creed, and why so much of his music sprang from literary influences — the biographer must delve back roughly a century before he took his first Sunday duty at St. Luke's, and travel northwards across the railwayless map of early 19th century England, continuing, after crossing the Border, towards the Edinburgh of 1819. There, on May 9th, his father Alexander Ireland was born of Fifeshire ancestry.

Alexander's own father's preoccupation was strictly business. From him the son inherited a sound commercial head. But from some other family strain came Alexander's intense interest in every aspect of the world of writers and writing.

Though his early years were geared to business interests, following in father's footsteps, Alexander also gathered around himself a nucleus of highly-gifted literary figures, whose friendship he won through enthusiastic studies and pursuits outside the realm of commerce. Each friendship led to another and more important contact, as when Dr John Gairdner, the Victorian medical reformer, introduced Ireland to the much more famous Emerson in 1833.

Ralph Waldo Emerson, to give the American-born poet, philosopher and essayist his full name, came to Europe for the first time in that year.

Gairdner's part in the temporary Anglicising of Emerson was to have been showing him round the tourist sights and literary sites of Edinburgh, but when his guest arrived, he realised how little freedom his practice actually left for revealing that city to an American thirsty for new experiences. Instead, Gairdner suggested that the bachelor Alexander Ireland should take Emerson under his wing, thus drawing Ireland for life into the Emerson—Carlyle circle.

In 1839, Alexander Ireland married Eliza Mary Blyth of Birmingham. It proved a tragically short union. Eliza Mary died only some three years later. Four years after this Alexander moved south, as a Huddersfield firm's resident representative in Manchester, the city that witnessed his rise to newspaper-world prosperity.

1846 was commercially Alexander Ireland's most important year, when he succeeded Edward Watkin — pioneer of leisure time for workers, and an early railway magnate — as business manager and publisher of the *Manchester Examiner.* The paper had been established only a year previously, as a rival to the *Manchester Guardian,* which was reckoned too unmindful, for some Mancunian tastes, of the North's fanatical anti-Corn Law league. After absorbing another local newspaper, the *Manchester Examiner* maintained for four decades a proud position as the city's second Press voice. As half-owner and editor of the *Examiner,* authoritative literary critic, expert on British writing in general, and possessor of a distinguished private library, Alexander Ireland's position as a literary leader was assured, and with it the continuing friendship of the famous. His home was an open house to eminent musicians and men of letters.

The third of the master writers who, with Emerson and Leigh Hunt, frequented Alexander Ireland's home, was

Carlyle, the Scot of lowly antecedents who, by sheer ability, made his way into Edinburgh University when only fifteen. When, in 1826, Carlyle married Jane Welsh — a fellow Scot, despite her surname — another fragment slotted into the jigsaw pattern of John Ireland's scholarly and musical heritage. Jane's shrewdness, wit, and talent as a letter-writer and author helped counter-balance her husband's forceful prose, and his attacks against the materialism and hypocrisy he considered prime evils of his generation.

Almost a quarter of a century of widowerhood elapsed before Alexander Ireland again said 'I will'. His new bride was Annie (in full, Anne Elizabeth) Nicholson, thirty years her husband's junior. Sister of an Aberdeen professor of natural history, Annie was herself a woman of uncommon intelligence for a period when woman's place was assumed to be in the home. Of no mean ability as an author and editor, she was mentally the ideal companion for a man of Alexander's intellect and station in life, able to converse on their own level with the writers and musicians who were always welcomed at the Ireland demesne.

Sounds of music and good conversation were, in due course, supplemented by sounds of childhood; crying, gurgling, playing. Alleyne, a son named after Annie's brother, was followed by three girls within the first half-decade of marriage. A seven-year gap intervened before the last child, John, arrived.

By this time the Irelands had made their home at 'Inglewood', a tall double-fronted Victorian house surrounded by pleasant gardens, at Bowdon in Cheshire. Bowdon was a much-favoured residential retreat of rich Manchester 'cotton-kings', and other powerful businessmen with large families and several servants. Their presence and carriage-class attendance put the place among Cheshire's most prosperous livings for the local clergy, hence a once common national saying, 'Not every man can be Vicar of Bowdon,' or top dog.

At Bowdon on August 13th, 1879, John Nicholson Ireland was born. His second baptismal appellation preserved his mother's maiden name. For the rest of his life John Ireland emphatically defended his birthplace against those who clung to its earlier spelling of Bowden despite evidence that, as early as Domesday Book, it was called Boge-don, a down (or hill) near a bog. Today's town motto is 'Beau Don' from a Norman-French pun, again emphasising that Bowdon, as Ireland insisted, was the correct spelling of his birthplace.

John Ireland was only three years old when the small happening occurred which became his first definite memory. It can be dated with fair accuracy from the fact that his father's old associate Emerson died in 1882, three years after young John, or 'Jackie', was born. During one of Emerson's last visits little Jackie toddled out into the garden and began grabbing up handfuls of daisies in the cheerfully haphazard manner of childhood. Probably his initial intention was to drop them into his loving mother's lap, but, on his way through the entrance hall, a more intriguing receptacle presented itself; a glossy top-hat lying upturned onto its crown like an open black vase. Into the hat went the daisies, Ireland recalled many years later. The topper was Emerson's.

Alexander Ireland was usually genial and hospitable to his guests, but a little remote-seeming to his children, on account of his grandfatherly rather than fatherly age. As he was about seventy when Jackie, the youngest, arrived, the boy naturally felt greater affinity with his mother who, according to nature's dictates, specially cherished the newest of her brood. Annie was a delicate but charming woman, suffering from angina, who spent almost as much time in her own pleasant room as in the main rooms downstairs, when no visitors were present, as was customary among ailing Victorian ladies of moderate to reasonable means.

Little Jackie spent hours in this sanctum with his musically-minded parent, whose piano playing was another of his earliest recollections. She, more than his journalistic father, instilled in him some instinct for rhythm and an appreciation of melody.

When dinner parties were given Jackie found fascination in the comings and goings of the drawing room and dining room. He was sometimes permitted to join the guests towards the end of the meal. Scarcely out of infancy, he thus became accustomed to looking up (literally), from his tiny pre-school stature, at great Victorians; men who included, as well as the usual parade of poets and authors, people of musical eminence. Sir Charles Hallé, founder of the Hallé Orchestra of Manchester, was among them.

Dame-school duly claimed the little boy. Like other six-and seven-year-olds of good social class, he endured the normal dame-school curriculum of 'Reading, 'Riting and 'Rithmetic'; but on many occasions Jackie and the others were released into the more appealing surroundings of Altrincham Park, a mile or so distant, taken there by a teacher for recreation and nature study. John Ireland derived enormous pleasure in old age, following radio and Press coverage of his 80th birthday celebrations, from a letter received from a lost contact of these infant days, asking whether he remembered those trips to Altrincham Park. From an equally venerable gentleman came a letter enclosing a snapshot group of the Bowdon dame-school boys in 1886, enquiring whether a dark, solemn-faced little chap in the front row was the same John Ireland he remembered as a fellow pupil. He was. This group is now in the comprehensive Ireland collection of his devoted friend and executrix, Norah Kirby, whose Sussex home, the John Ireland Memorial House, is an enthralling unofficial museum devoted to memories, records and documents appertaining to the composer.

During the 1880's Jackie's father's fortunes suffered a serious but not disastrous setback which the modern Press, through newspaper and magazine articles, and musical reviews, has tended to exaggerate. When Liberal support for the *Manchester Examiner* was transferred to the rival *Manchester Guardian,* which had gained much support in the light of Gladstone's home-rule proposals, the *Examiner's* readership — and profits — fell sharply. After merging temporarily with another publication the paper slid into oblivion. Alexander Ireland, by then an octogenarian, is recorded as having borne this worrying period 'with great dignity and fortitude'. The hardest personal blow was the sale of the best editions from his magnificent and valuable private library, including 17th century editions of Burton's classic *Anatomy of Melancholy.*

The Irelands were down, but not out. Their fortunes never dipped so low as sensationalism has implied. Standards had to be lowered, and assets pruned, but a reasonable degree of comfort and social position was left. John's 'poverty' as a music student, assumed because of his father's reversals, was never the starvation-in-a-garret affair, à *La Bohème*, which has been implied. The chief repercussion upon the family was a move from 'Inglewood' at Bowdon — a house requiring expensive upkeep and staffing — into a smaller home at Southport on the west coast.

Probably of more immediate effect on the youngest Ireland child than these financial upheavals and changes of habitat, were the generation gaps within his closest circle, growing more pronounced as time passed. Firstly, between himself and the youngest of his big sisters came a seven-year break. Several more years came between John and his only brother; enormous gulfs in the mind of a child. Infinitely larger was the gulf between Jackie at seven and his father at seventy-seven. A well-preserved Blackpool seaside photographer's effort of 1886 portrays it better than words can possibly do. A fragile-looking small boy stands half frightened by the studio paraphernalia, beside a moustached septuagenarian who, if one were not told otherwise, could be assumed to be his grandfather, or even great-grandfather. This historic picture, in case John Ireland no longer possessed a copy, was sent to him shortly before his death in 1962 by his childhood friend Helen, who will be encountered again later in this chapter.

Even Jackie's mother, though thirty years Alexander's junior, was not like his school chums' more girlish mamas, much though he loved her and much though she adored her final chick. Inevitably, as the offspring of ageing parents, one of whom was semi-invalid, he came under the rule of big-brother Alleyne and the three girls for immediate punishment of infantile misdeeds and occasional administrations of what, further south, would be termed a leathering.

The thing that brought him real repose and happiness was music, encouraged by both parents. As they grew up the girls took good piano lessons, preparing them for future serious study, and Annie Ireland, though primarily a writer, also loved music deeply; constant contact with good music and good books were for Jackie natural facts of life. He showed genuine interest in the piano by the age of eight, and began composing simple tunes long before taking any formal tuition in that art.

Following periods of schooling at Colwyn Bay and elsewhere, young Ireland went on to Leeds Grammar School. An incident during this Yorkshire interlude left so vivid a memory with one woman that after Ireland became famous she was inspired to pass it on to Percy Scholes, editor of the *Oxford Companion to Music.* Scholes accepted — and printed — this as Ireland's earliest recorded public performance, playing Raff's once almost embarrassingly popular *Cavatina* on the piano of a Harrogate hotel.

Ireland's own recollections of his elementary piano training were amusingly made public in his maturity during one of the BBC's long-running *Music Magazine* programmes. The process was tersely described as 'Beethoven . . . approached through punishment and the key of G.' Punishment, because a rap on the knuckles was a perfectly normal chastisement from a teacher; and the key of G because piano teachers everywhere introduced children first to the 'open' key of C (no sharps or flats to learn), followed by work in the two next easiest keys of F (one flat) and G (one sharp). Many of the best elementary teaching pieces being by Beethoven, and written in that master's much-favoured key of G (some of the *Bagatelles* and *Sonatinas,* the easiest early short *Sonata,* and the unavoidable *Minuet in G*), little John Ireland for some considerable time believed that all Beethoven's music was in G.

Annie Ireland, John's mother, might have been physically fragile, plagued by a heart weakness which killed her soon after he entered his teens; but mentally she kept alert and creative. In 1891 she brought out the authoritative biography of Jane Welsh Carlyle, wife of the Irelands' famous friend Thomas, Jane having achieved enough in her own right to merit a life history for public consumption. So entertaining and informative was Jane Carlyle's correspondence over the years with another literary friend, so alive with comment on people and events of the fast-moving mid-Victorian era, that her letters deserved publication as social documents of human and historical interest. It was Annie Ireland who edited them, brilliantly, for issue a few years before the 19th century ended.

By the opening of the nineties, John Ireland had decided

11

that music meant more to him than to the average youth, expected by his parents to acquire an 'accomplishment' such as piano or singing. Music would be his future life and living. It was no passing schoolboy whim, but an irreversible decision in making what Dr. Johnson called 'the Choice of Life'.

Obviously the next step towards becoming a concert pianist, his initial goal, was to seek more serious training. He must aim high, at London itself. But was he good enough? Could he get into Britain's premier training grounds purely on merit, without recommendation? The only way to find out was to try — unaided.

Reminiscing in his eighties, John Ireland vividly recalled the test of character as well as of piano technique which he voluntarily put himself through as a sensitive provincial boy. As it was retold to the author:

'Early in 1893 the thirteen-year-old John Ireland told his mother of his desire to study music and become a concert pianist. Then without telling anyone of his intentions he took himself to London, via Manchester, to have an audition at the Royal College of Music. This he passed with flying colours, and was accepted as a full-time student to commence his piano studies in the summer term with Mr. Frederick Cliffe.' Ireland entered the College not at fourteen, as is often stated, but even more amazingly at only thirteen, a few months before his fourteenth birthday.

Annie Ireland was by then very much an invalid whose worsening heart condition required freedom from stress and worry. Doubtless this was why the thoughtful boy told her nothing in advance of his proposed long, unaccompanied journey to London, and of his important audition, though the effect on her health had his disappearance been discovered before he was safely home again would surely have been severe.

In the event his absence went unnoticed, thanks to possession of a season ticket to a Manchester exhibition of motor-engines, acquired by his father as a perk of his newspaper connections. John, crazy about motors and motoring, had already been every day and stayed until closing time. He was therefore assumed to be spending yet another whole day at the show; enough, with careful planning, to cover his return London journey and audition.

All went smoothly. Home again, John straightaway confessed his escapade to Mrs. Ireland. Once recovered from the initial shock, pride cancelled out most of her instinct to scold: pride not only at his winning a place in one of Britain's top colleges on his own merit, but also pride in his initiative. His determination to study seriously, she realised, was unshakeable. His acceptance at so tender an age confirmed that he possessed above-average talent, worthy of the best training.

Impressed, and probably conscious that her deteriorating condition might well prevent her seeing John make his mark, Annie Ireland made a quick decision. To quote again:

'She, realising his determination to study music, settled a sum of money on him to produce a sufficient income to cover his college fees and living costs in the simple luxury of lodgings in houses kept by gentlewomen with small incomes, supplemented by letting rooms'. Young Ireland certainly had to count his pennies, like all students; but, thanks to his prudent mother and, later, extra income from his father's estate, he did not suffer the privations of true poverty which have been read into his college days, on the assumption that loss of a parent, student life, and penury automatically went together.

John was comparatively fortunate in being neither alone in London, nor forced into sharing 'digs' with uncongenial strangers. The youngest of the three Ireland girls, now almost a young woman, was already studying the piano at the establishment known flippantly to Royal College of Music students hailing from Up North simply as 't'other place'; properly, the Royal Academy of Music. She had most satisfactory lodgings with separate bedrooms and a sitting room/study, in Bayswater, a by-no-means unattractive quarter of the metropolis. Ireland's life in lodgings, as recounted to the present writer, continued:

'Another bedroom being available, the boy rented that, and shared the sitting room and all meals with his sister and the "delightful" resident cat, with whom he (a lifelong cat lover) immediately made friends, and never forgot.'

13

Seven decades later Ireland could still describe this feline friend, doyenne of a long line of landladies' cats, friends' cats, and casually encountered cats, which runs as steadily through his life story as the bass-line of a Bach passacaglia.

Talking in retrospect of all the student lodgings that followed, he invariably ended his account with: 'And there was such a nice cat there.' Or a 'delightful' cat, his favourite word for any creature that took time off from washing to purr for him. Its coat markings, mannerisms, battle scars, the set of its tail — or lack of a tail, if it had lost a disagreement with a London cab — were crystal clear in his mind's eye at the age of eighty. As one who knew him intimately summed up: 'He never forget a cat, or what he looked like.'

Pedigree Siamese, or household pets making up in character what they lacked in show-cage awards, were alike to John Ireland. From his first landlady's cat to the ginger tom who merited his favourite adjective of 'delightful' by gladdening his last Sussex drives in old age, he rarely, if ever, failed to pass the time of day with any furry presence that crossed his path.

At college Ireland wholeheartedly followed his pre-determined course towards a career as a concert pianist, under his tutor Frederick Cliffe. From Cliffe he imbibed the understanding and sympathy for this popular but somewhat percussive instrument which was reflected in his output after he turned to composition. Few knew better than the maturing Ireland how to make a piano sing, murmer like winds, or sweep like waves.

The future seemed bright and reasonably predictable when fate struck one of those cruel blows which she appears deliberately to keep in hand for mortals whose courses seem seem set too fair. Soon after he came to London his beloved mother's heart failed her, on October, 4th, 1893, less than six months after John became a music student. Her attainments as a writer were recognised by the *Manchester Guardian*, whose prosperity had helped extinguish her husband's *Manchester Examiner*. The *Guardian's* account of Annie's life, published some time after her death, formed a main basis for her entry in the *Dictionary of National Biography*, immediately following the entry about her husband.

Fate had not yet finished with young John Ireland. Not long after Annie's death, just before the Christmas of 1894, Alexander joined her in the Hereafter, from his final earthly home at Mauldeth Road, Withington. The boy, at only fourteen, was now an orphan.

Remote though Alexander Ireland may have seemed, and despite their disparity in years, he was still a father and family figurehead. His loss cut the final link between John's old life and the new. Financially, John now became dependant upon two guardians whose mutual creed was the solid Victorian motto 'Waste not, want not.'

John's actual share of his father's assets worked out at two-sixteenths of the estate's value. The elder brother and the three sisters, virtually young women, inherited twice as much, a quarter each. John's share was left in trust until the lad came of age.

The guardians were both lawyers. As a result they conducted affairs between themselves and their charge more like interviews in an attorney's office than personal encounters with a young lad who, having lost both parents at the outset of his studies, needed adult sympathy and advice, as well as kindly shoulders to lean on in confidence when times seemed black or studies went badly. One lived a safe distance away, at Brighton; the other was uncomfortably close, at Hampstead in North London. Every weekend this business-like gentleman, at whose Finchley Road home the lad was required to dine rather uncomfortably, calculated the next seven days' estimated expenditure, worked out with scant regard either for unexpected expenses or the small pleasures that mean so much to a teenager. To quote Norah Kirby, companion of his latter years, whose account based on the composer's own fireside remembrances cannot be bettered:

'Each Sunday his London guardian carefully calculated his expenditure (on College fees, rooms with service, and all meals) for the coming week, and gave him a sufficient sum to cover it, making him enter every item of expenditure into a black leather account book, to be scrutinised before the following Sunday's luncheon, after which he gave the boy his usual weekly allowance. This meant that "luxuries" were

15

condemned as extravagance, and deducted from the following week's allowance.'

The handing-over process was usually accompanied by a grim little lecture on thrift.

Every pre-decimalised ha'penny spent must be accounted for in that black book of reckoning. *Two* pen-nibs? Would not one nib do, and the cheapest in the shop instead of second cheapest? Oh, *indeed;* so one was for music and one for ordinary writing; surely music could be written with the same implement as a note beginning 'Dear Aunt . . . Thank you for your lovely birthday gift?' John Ireland had to speak convincingly to explain exactly why two nibs were different.

These weekly sums, once agreed and doled out, enabled John at first to board with his sister Ethel. Periodically they changed quarters, in favour of increased privacy, better practice space, or closer proximity to their respective Colleges. Coming to roost near Paddington Station, Ethel and John invited one of Ethel's RAM friends to join them, sharing the rental; a harpist with whom came a small niece left in the older girl's care. The former *menage-à-deux* was now a happy foursome, occupying, thanks to pooled funds, a comfortable three-bedroomed home with a large studio-cum-sitting-room, ideal for music practice as well as relaxation.

At sixteen, John risked the shocking extravagance of treating the harpist's niece Helen to a bicycle, which he taught her to ride by 'running behind her, holding the back of the saddle'. Weeks of scrimping and saving tiny amounts, which hopefully would not rouse suspicion, went into Helen's bicycle fund. Yet we know, from Helen's own memories as an octogenarian, that the John of this period, despite his guardians' constrictions and intensifying college study, could still strike her as 'the merriest boy she ever knew'. He was cheery enough by nature not to adopt any falsely introspective pose in the belief that a budding classical musician ought to show himself superior to ordinary mortals, who knew not B-flat from a bull's flat foot. Laughing and talking, he regularly took Helen down by penny horse-bus to Buzzard's emporium in Oxford Street for half an hour's giggling over the biggest ice-creams he could afford. Even in this juvenile activity a small pointer to the future can be seen; Helen usually chose girlish strawberry-pink ices but John, eschewing 'cissy' pink, settled for a delicate pale green variety of water-ice, suggesting that even before the nineties were out he liked a certain lovely colour between leaf-green and jade. Today, correspondence from the John Ireland Trust, and official lists of his works and recordings, are usually printed on paper whose hue might be unofficially christened John Ireland Green.

Of the ice-cream jaunts John's guardians certainly became disapprovingly aware. He was 'severely reprimanded' and lectured on the sins of self-indulgence and of spending on non-necessities. But lectures could not take away the happiness which those 'wasted' pence had bought for himself and a little girl in the crowded loneliness of Victorian London.

With the money prudently settled on him by his mother, plus the dole out of his father's estate, John Ireland was not condemned to anything approaching true poverty. Nevertheless, extra shillings were always useful for bridging the difference between adequate existence and minor luxuries. The greatest thing about fees earned by acting as accompanist to fellow students and others, at the smoking-concerts which were such a prominent feature of 19th century musical activity, was that 'the money was his *own*, to spend as he wished', without accusations about squandering cash on fripperies, by his formidable legal custodians. The fee for a smoking-concert was all of five shillings (25p) for an evening's demanding but enjoyable playing. Five 'bob' could make a fellow 'feel passing rich'.

Ireland also took Sunday organ duties at various churches, likewise for useful small fees. A second study instrument being obligatory in most musical colleges, Ireland had chosen the organ. Already he was sensitive enough to the inner heart of music to take a church for the excellence of its organ, rather than the size of the offered stipend.

For organ study at College, Ireland came under tutelage of Sir Walter Parratt, the celebrated organist of St. George's Chapel at Windsor, one of the topmost appointments in the land. Often, when famous himself, Ireland looked back to the occasion when he, a knickerbockered stripling, took the unheard-of step of standing up to this great man.

17

Parratt's habit of allowing groups of girl students into his sanctum whilst giving lessons was naturally extremely disconcerting to a sensitive lad. His embarrassment, cruelly, was increased by the thoughtlessness of Parratt himself. 'Look at his boots!' chortled the professor in his reedy voice (Ireland, at about fourteen, was 'still in knickerbockers, stockings and boots'). Next moment, chameleon-like, Parratt became the august professor again: 'Now, *Mr.* Ireland; I want you to improvise,' he demanded. John played not one note, pleading unconvincingly: 'Yes, Sir; but I would rather not, if you don't mind . . . I . . . I . . . I don't feel very well today.' Prudence saved him from blurting out the real truth; that a gaggle of giggling girls, waiting to witness his first fistful of 'dominoes' — as musicians everywhere term wrong notes — was so unnerving that even Parratt's wrath was preferable. 'Sit down at once, and improvise!' thundered the master, accustomed to total obedience. Ireland obstinately repeated, 'I really don't feel very well.' Parratt offered one last chance, with a contemptuous dig at Ireland's youth in his tone of address: 'Now, MISTER Ireland, will you, or will you not, improvise?' Ireland refused boldly, answering, 'No Sir, I will NOT!' a feat requiring no small amount of courage. Parratt pronounced his ultimatum: 'If you disobey me, you will leave this room at once — and never come back to it again.' Ireland went.

Though Ireland, in defying a man like Parratt, had broken every rule of etiquette between pupil and master, the two were ultimately reconciled. Ireland continued his organ studies in the privacy that should have been any learner's right, minus female chorus.

Music apart, the happiest period of Ireland's college days was when the four friends — John and Ethel Ireland, Helen and her harpist aunt — took lodgings in a gracious Victorian house in Sunningdale Gardens, Kensington. Long after he became independent, modestly famous, and owner of a proper studio, Ireland visited his particular ex-landlady as a friend, and to have words with her 'friendly, much-loved tabby cat'. As has been said before, and will be said again, Ireland was among modern music's leading felinophiles. To him, all cats certainly did not look alike.

His sixteenth year was an eventful one. Indeed, he had not quite reached that birthday when he won his FRCO (Fellowship of the Royal College of Organists), the youngest student recipient of the award up to that time.

At fifteen, Ireland decided for himself that composition rather than concert performance was his true bent. He was still under sixteen when he wrote without formal tuition the two piano pieces entitled *Daydream* and *Meridian,* which were reckoned worthy of publication many years later.

It is not easy, when scanning any musical dictionary, to find many composers of late 19th century origin without the repetitive tag, 'studied under Stanford'. Ireland was not a Stanford pupil at this point, but at the College he idolised and idealised the Irishman, and nursed a burning ambition to join those studying composition under him. Typically, he set about accomplishing his dream on his own initiative. Several times he boldly accosted Stanford in the corridors, asking to join his class. 'We'll see, me b'hoy; we'll see' was all he could get out of him. It seemed like a challenge to produce something good enough to *make* Stanford see his ability.

Instead of forgetting music, Ireland therefore devoted much of his 1895 summer holiday in the Lake District, with Ethel and Evlyn Howard-Jones (dedicatee of the aforementioned piano pieces), to work on his first string quartet, though the only composition tuition he had received so far was the elementary exercises normally incorporated into study of an instrument.

He was shocked, stunned, and deeply hurt when, after knocking on Stanford's door at the College and holding out his beautifully written score with a shy 'For you Sir; I have written this for *you*,' his Irish-accented hero bluntly brushed the offering aside. With stinging brusqueness he commented, 'Dull as ditchwater, me b'hoy. Take it away.' John never remembered how he got out of that room, except that he 'shut the door very quietly'.

Stanford revised his opinion on less hasty second thoughts. His expert eye must have taken in more than Ireland realised. Relenting — possibly feeling a trifle guilty about his cruelly abrupt refusal of the lad's tribute to himself — Stanford arranged for a public performance in due course by four student string players, at a College pupils' concert.

While John Ireland's quartet was being played, a distinguished professorial figure slipped in and stopped, listening intently. He was none other than Sir Hubert Parry, Director of the Royal College of Music. A man of Parry's stature need not sit through an entire quartet to form an opinion. Near the end of the opening movement he appeared to enquire who the composer was. Somebody pointed in Ireland's direction. Without waiting for more, Parry walked up to the young composer, sitting at the back of the hall, tapped him on the shoulder, and quietly remarked: 'Capital my boy! Capital!' Then followed the words that delighted Ireland: 'You are a *composition* scholar.'

Next day John Ireland tackled Stanford again. This time, one suspects, his eyes glinted with the mischief that was characteristic of him when coming out with something unmaliciously wicked: 'Sir! I'm a composition scholar. Will you take me *now*!'

Ireland worked with his hero from 1897 to 1901, thus earning the standard biographical entry for his generation, 'studied under Stanford'.

The list of Stanford's other students of the time makes revealing reading. As well as Ireland, they included Frank Bridge, Rutland Boughton (of *Immortal Hour* fame), Gustav Holst, George Dyson (*The Canterbury Pilgrims*) and Ralph Vaughan Williams.

The first quartet was only recently published, and found to be remarkably accomplished considering the writer's youth. Another followed a year later. He never wrote a quartet in full manhood.

In 1896 was announced a vacancy of special interest to all London's more ambitious organists, at Holy Trinity, Sloane Street. Knowing that this church owned a singularly fine organ, Ireland applied for an audition. He won on merit, against applicants far older than his seventeen years. As the author's confidante, Norah Kirby, confirmed, 'the salary was infinitesimal', but with his independent income he could just afford not to care; 'his only thought was that he would be able to play such a magnificent organ', and control a specially fine choir.

Ireland began upon his small output of church music at about this time, with a setting of the Office of Holy Communion in A-flat for boys' voices with organ. It was withdrawn, unpublished, with much other work composed before about 1906.

In 1898 he acquired his first real home, as opposed to lodgings, a flat in Elm Park Mansions, Chelsea. There he installed some newly acquired pieces of antique furniture, foreshadowing a permanent interest. At his death he still owned these original Chelsea pieces.

At Elm Park was written one of Ireland's most important and unusual early works; an *Intermezzo* (or *Sextet*) for clarinet, horn and string quartet. No work is known to have been written for this piquant instrumental combination before.

History repeated itself. The Stanford who rejected the quartet written for him in sincere schoolboy admiration was the Stanford who disliked the *Sextet* for its 'flavour of Brahms'; Brahms, being still alive, was the idol of young musicians. Though he bothered to have the manuscript bound, the dispirited creator shut it into a drawer, where it lay for 62 long years, unplayed. Not until 1960, shortly before his death, was Ireland persuaded to allow a performance at a Hampton Music Club concert. Was Stanford right? Actions spoke louder than words as a verdict when, directly after the performance, a leading publisher begged to be allowed to issue it to the public.

An anecdote underlying this work's resurrection perfectly illustrates how the astonishing musicianship of great men is often preserved into old age. When the clarinettist Thea King went to run through another Ireland work with him, she asked, on the spur of the moment: 'Have you written anything else for clarinet?' Casually he answered, with the customary preceding 'Oh' whose tones cannot be reproduced in printer's ink: 'Oh, yes; there's an old work in that drawer I wrote at the age of 18 . . . you can have it if you like.' He offered to go through it with her. During supper with Ireland's companion Norah Kirby (he, old and tired with his exertions, had excused himself with a supper tray upstairs) Thea King remarked: 'You had me up the garden path about his sight.' 'What do you mean?' asked the one who knew

21

better than any the extent of his semi-blindness, and had instructed the clarinettist to put all questions into singing, or to play them at the piano, as he could not possibly read a score. But Ireland, analysing the music stage by stage, had remarked every pitfall, each point of phrasing, and recalled every instrumental part — entirely from memory, after six decades. Thea King's astonishment was not lessened when he merely said: *'Anybody* could do *that*! It's all *here'* (pointing to his forehead). Anybody, of course, could never perform the memory feats of the Irelands of this world.

When Walter Alcock, principal Holy Trinity organist, left for Westminster Abbey, where his name became synonymous with majestic music for State occasions, Ireland hoped to rise from assistant organist into the vacant post. But the church council considered him, still under-age, too youthful to take full charge of this important town-church, and appointed an older man. The disappointed Ireland, however, was offered the consolation prize of St. Jude's, Chelsea, Holy Trinity's daughter church.

Traditionally, the youngsters of a church are the responsibility of the curate and organist; the curate because he himself is usually only just out of theological college; the organist because, regardless of age, he is accustomed to handling and understanding small boys. St. Jude's and Holy Trinity treated their choirboys well. Other churches and Sunday Schools took their children on the day outings known as treats, comprising games and races in some nearby open space reached by horse-brake, followed by disappearing acts involving large quantities of eatables. These London choristers did rather better. Each year the organist and curate escorted them on a complete fortnight's seaside holiday, charged to return them home with limbs intact. A local school, closed for summer holidays, was rented as dormitory accommodation. From this HQ the two men took their charges by charabanc for country drives, or on bathing and boating expeditions.

Deal and Herne Bay, in Kent, were among resorts honoured by the London merrymakers. Another year they descended on Worthing in Sussex, though Ireland never dreamed then that the county he fell in love with on drives would prove to be his final home. Nor did he guess that one

22

of his topographical 'love affairs' was beginning when the next curate, a Channel Islander, suggested transferring the annual spree to his native shores; nor that the Islands would cast such a spell as to influence his thinking, inspire some of his best music, and spark off a passion for everything prehistoric. John Ireland went to Jersey as a choristers' courier; he returned fascinated by the Islands and their lore.

1900 was a personal as well as a universal landmark year. At twenty-one, officially of age, he was freed of his guardians and gained control of his full share of Alexander Ireland's estate. He would never need to compose hack-work for the sake of a living: 'everything he wrote was what he felt impelled to write'. At about the same time he became organist-choirmaster of St. Luke's, Chelsea in addition to St. Jude's. He stayed there for a quarter of a century, and Chelsea remained his home and parish almost for life. His only regret was loss of his glorious old Holy Trinity organ, which he considered the organist's *beau-ideal* compared with St. Luke's somewhat indifferent pipework. At over eighty he often woke from one of those recurrent dreams which haunt some sleepers for years, exclaiming: 'I was having such a happy dream. I was back playing the organ at Holy Trinity — and it was so *wonderful!*'

Settled into Chelsea, Ireland left Elm Park for a studio in nearby Gunter Grove, taking his antiques with him. There he passed his most prolific years as a composer, and took many pupils. The enrolment of one of these illustrates Ireland's innate kindness, displayed when still only in his early twenties. Arriving late for choir-practice one evening, he found Cantorus I (the leading boy) sitting in his own place at the piano, playing the instrument himself. Unknown to his choirmaster young Charles Markes, Cantorus I, had taught himself to play on the black notes when aged only four, attracted by their sound (a progression which, incidentally, much appealed to Ireland himself as a composer). Charles could read music properly at seven, and accompany an uncle in operatic arias at eight. Once Charles began, on the occasion in question, to play through next Sunday's music, the others gathered instinctively round him. Soon an enthusiastic unofficial choir practice was in full swing. The singing subsided like the proverbial pricked balloon when Ireland, possessed of the master musician's natural ability to create a cessation of hubbub merely by entering a gathering of players or singers, suddenly walked in and, after hanging up his favourite astrakhan—collared coat, remarked: 'When you have quite finished, Charles, perhaps we may begin?' Cantorus I shrank into the ranks, but did not escape being called back after-wards with an ominous-sounding 'Charlie, I want you', for a Dutch Uncle talk. Finding that the lad lived close by in Cheyne Walk, Ireland insisted on walking home with him, to the boy's consternation. Presumably he intended reporting his behaviour to Mother. It certainly seemed like it when Ireland bluntly went to the point: 'I've brought your son home. What are you going to *do* about him?' But the ques-tion had a totally different meaning. Ireland had recognised outstanding promise in this eight-year-old child's playing. 'He's a heaven-born pianist,' Ireland continued; 'Are you go-ing to have him taught?' Mother, a widow with two boys, professed herself unable to afford favouring one without the other. 'Oh, I *see*,' commented Ireland. And he *did* see the only answer to unmoneyed talent. 'Oh well, I suppose I'll just have to teach him myself.' Next day Charlie — or Charles, in full — was summoned to tea with his organist-choirmaster, when the child's inborn musicianship was discussed and put to the test. The promised lessons began soon afterwards.

Destiny called again in about 1904 when Ireland met Elgar at the home of Basil Nevinson, the cellist 'B.G.N.' of the *Enigma* 'Friends Pictured Within'. Speaking of his urge to make good as a composer, Ireland received from Elgar a piece of personal advice: 'I believe you are going to be a composer. Do you expect to make a *living* from composition, Mr. Ireland?' 'Yes sir,' the young man answered. 'Then God help you! Look at *me*! I've been composing for years, yet no-one in England took any notice of me till a *German* (Richard Strauss) told 'em to!' This, of course, was the day when any musician whose name did not end with -ovitch or -auss was automatically reckoned second rate, compelling even Henry Wood to call himself Klenovsky to get an unbiassed hearing.

Independence was a heady sensation for a young fellow put in charge of his own assets. Times were past when 12s. 6d.

(62½p) 'blown' on a shiny top-hat, which the 16-year-old Holy Trinity sub-organist had felt was essential sartorial equipment for playing at weddings, brought sour accusations of 'enormous extravagance' from a guardian who paid 10s. 6d. (52½p) for his own headgear, and docked the offending extra 2s. (10p) from the following week's allowance.

Significantly, the catalogue of Ireland's surviving works springs to life at about the time of his majority. We find listed his earliest unison song, *The Frog and the Crab* (1900); a *Berceuse* for violin of 1902; and the more important cycle, *Songs of a Wayfarer* written in about 1903—4. Here emerges an inborn judgement in matching the right poetry to the right music, dating from childhood immersion in literature. Each song is set to a different poet, from Shakespeare to Rossetti and Blake, yet each complements the other exactly. Singers still enjoy the exciting *Spleen* (poem by Ernest Dowson), and good accompanists its technical complexities.

More than half Ireland's surprisingly small organ output, considering his love for this instrument, dates from the 20th century's opening: *Elegiac Romance* (1902); *Villanella* (1904) a *Cavatina*, afterwards withdrawn, and a suite ending with a swinging *Marcia Popolare*. Two unpublished items of church music deserve mention, a *Paternoster*, or Lord's Prayer, and his sole Anglican chant. He was also probably working on the *Te Deum* of the Morning Service known according to standard church nomenclature simply as *Ireland in F*; the other sections were added later. This service was dedicated 'To the Choristers of St. Luke's, Chelsea.' They were choristers he would not forget, nor would they forget him, as he became increasingly famous.

One alone remains today; Charles Markes, the Charlie of the choir-practice incident. This ex-chorister, in his seventies, today inhabits the same London area a few minutes from Gunter Grove where much of Ireland's best music was written. To his reminiscences of Ireland's middle and most productive years the author owes a considerable debt.

St. Luke's, in a sense, has a double existence today: in reality, down near the Thames; and in the blue-grey imagery of John Ireland's memorial window in the City.

3. Many Waters Cannot Quench Love

Under the cameo of Ireland wearing the robes of a Doctor of Music the opening bars of his magnificent anthem *Greater Love Hath No Man* (known equally well from its first line as *Many Waters Cannot Quench Love*), can be clearly read in the Musicians' Chapel window.

This famous example of early 20th century church music represents the full flowering of Ireland's creative genius. It is the earliest of those works which are familiar to the general public, marking the establishment of contact between the composer and Everyman instead of only between himself and a knowledgeable professional circle.

Between his coming of age at twenty-one and the composition of *Greater Love* at about thirty-three, Ireland established himself more firmly in the local and district life of Chelsea. He was free of the restrictions of guardianship and, with his father's bequest as support; free to teach and compose in his own quarters, to entertain friends, and to enjoy liberal pints and more liberal laughter with cronies in the nearby Gunter Arms.

Although chamber music still attracted him the new century seemed to inspire in him, as in other perceptive creative artists, an urge to burst new bounds of ideas. Musicians began looking forward and started to climb off safe melodic band-wagons to hitch rides on less predictable but more exciting vehicles. Ireland's *Sextet* well illustrates a composer re-thinking four-square Victorian tradition into a new mould; it also demonstrates again that streak of self-confident determination that sent a thirteen-year-old child to a big London audition alone. This work was born — or, rather, re-conceived — from a failed orchestral piece killed off by a critical

Stanford at College: 'Well ... Y'see, me b'hoy, it won't *do*. .. You'll have to try again.'

> If at first you don't succeed,
> Try, try, try again.

It seems unthinkable that Annie Ireland would have failed to drum into the young Jackie this universal Victorian blueprint for future success in life. So John Ireland *did* try again. His conventional orchestra of full strings, woodwind and brass shrank to a string quartet, with only one woodwind instrument, the clarinet with whose sound he had recently fallen in love after hearing a recital of Brahms' sonatas, and one of brass, the French horn which echoed in his brain following a performance by the man for whom Brahms wrote his *Horn Trio,* whose first English performance Ireland heard. 'What a lovely combination!' thought Ireland, with the timbre of these two instruments in mind. The result was transformation of an unconvincing traditional orchestral exercise into an unusual and convincing chamber work, the first ever written for this particular ensemble.

This, incidentally, was not Ireland's only reduction of an orchestral piece down to chamber proportions. Another, carefully bound, is in the British Museum; a *Poem in A-minor.*

All at once Ireland found himself on the threshold of recognition; celebrating the throwing off of guardianship and of minority by taking up motoring when public allegiance was still to the bicycle and the horse; graduating as Bachelor of Music of Durham University (1905) and settling into two aspects of Chelsea life — the organist-choirmastership of St. Luke's, which he was destined to hold for the next twenty-two years, and the more extrovert life of Chelsea's strong artistic community. He welcomed a host of acquaintances to Gunter Grove to eat, drink and discuss music. They ranged from choristers and pupils to sculptors and painters. Best of all were those times when just one or two came in, to chat or simply sit and think. Then 'The Studio' lived up to the late Sir Eugene Goossens' description: 'the quiet haven of a few intimate friends'. Goossens came to know the man and his music so closely that in later life he could declare: 'A lifelong friendship with him has been a rewarding experience. If the humility and artistic sincerity of a modest artist find their best expression in that artist's work, then John Ireland's contains the deepest known to me.'

Ireland was a man of contrasts, even more marked in these heady young Chelsea days than in old age. Small and slight of stature, he was big-hearted as a home entertainer or as a convivial patron of the bar at the Chelsea Arts Club; a church organist but of somewhat unorthodox Christianity; capable of suddenly switching from several hours' religious argument to Arts Club cheerfulness, even rakishness; a man needing quietness for creative ends, yet equally happy sputtering around on his motorcycle or, later, in his first motor car. The latter was his most 'extravagant' investment after throwing off the shackles of his guardian's weekly dole, bought from an inheritance now at last under his own control. As if to symbolise visibly his freedom and youth, he displayed exuberance in his choice of motorised transport: a green Talbot 8 with cheery yellow-painted wings. In the Talbot — forerunner of a string of cars — Ireland delighted to explore London at its best, free of wagons and commercial chaos, between Sunday services.

14 Gunter Grove was ideally placed for the Chelsea Arts Club, and those places of public resort to whose crowded bars the musical and artistic fraternity assembled as much for the company as the beer. Ireland's 'local' could not have been more local; the Gunter Arms (familiarly, the Gunter) on the corner.

Much though he enjoyed London, and Chelsea in particular, Ireland had equal affection for the sea and countryside. With his little car he could explore the beauty spots of Dorset, West Sussex and the North Downs on day trips. Having the fortunate combination of income from his parents' settlements, teaching fees, his St. Luke's stipend, and extra fees for weddings and funerals, he could now afford to spend longer sojourns out of town, most of which brought forth ideas for translating into music. His hymn tune *Eastergate,* published in 1906, is a reminder that he took a room for weekends in a cottage at Eastergate in Sussex. The owners who 'did for' their guest were charming, and the village, not far from Plumpton racecourse, was as yet innocent of a main road.

Of greater significance in critical circles was the *Phantasie*

Trio written in the year before *Eastergate* but not published until two years later, in 1908. It was inspired by Jersey. The composer's developing 'love affair' with the Channel Islands, Guernsey in particular, could best be expressed in his most fluent medium, music. As in reality, the island's rocky coast appears and disappears through clouds of spuming spray — dotted notes — and its waves surge in the musical undercurrents which became typical of much of his future descriptive music, eddying underneath the melody.

E. J. Moeran, Ireland's pupil and friend, looking back from 1923 with knowledge of his actual development, put the *Phantasie's* transitional nature into a nutshell when he wrote:

'For seven years after his studentship came to an end in 1901, he produced nothing which he consider(ed) representative of himself. The turning point came in 1908 with the *A-Minor Phantasy-trio,* which was awarded a prize in the Cobbett Competition and subsequently published. Even by this time he had been unable to throw off entirely the squareness and pomposity induced by his early associations, although this work reveals a certain transition in style.'

That transition, from a composer feeling his way out of college-bred traditionalism towards a more modern and personal idiom, came about in the summer of the *Phantasie Trio's* natal year (1906) in a noisy, steamy, crowded, unmusical and most unlikely place — a platform on Charing Cross Station in London.

The composer was bound for another favourite retreat, the calm small seaside resort of Deal, where he had taken a flat in the picturesque High Street. He made frequent visits from London on a slow, but pretty, Kentish ride by steam train from Charing Cross. Waiting one day on the platform for his train to arrive he wandered across to one of the newspaper and book kiosks which then stood on the actual platforms as well as on the main concourse. He was not looking for anything in particular, but one book immediately caught his casual eye and held it as if two contacts had fused together. The cover was unusual, extremely striking, and out of the normal run of railway-bookstall stock. So was its title, *The*

House of Souls (not *The Hills of Dreams*, as is sometimes stated; this title was not published until a year later). The book 'sold itself' to the passing idler, who had had no intention of buying.

Dipping into *The House of Souls*, Ireland felt an immediate affinity with the Welshman, Machen, whose name rhymed with the Welsh or Teutonic 'bach' and whose writings have been succinctly categorised as 'mystical, macabre, romantic'. But Machen's romance was far removed from normal Charing Cross bookstall tales of boy-meets-girl. His brand of romance was the fey, strange world of extremest antiquity, the occult, and happenings inexplicable in everyday terms.

Ireland already had an interest in ancient races and rites and in prehistoric sites, which was immediately inflamed by what Masefield has called 'those beautiful and terrible stories'. Machen's strange tales of mystics of the silent hills, whose counterparts even existed for those like himself who possessed inward eyes to detect them in mundane Holborn, went with the sureness of arrows to Ireland's mind. They affected his musical thinking, off and on, for life. He bought every other available Machen book and every new title as it appeared including the next in line, *The Hill of Dreams* (1907), whose horrifying evil aura clinging to an ancient fort probably influenced Ireland's great orchestral masterpiece, *Mai-Dun*.

Machen's magical, misty, eerie pre-history, which Ireland dubbed a 'racial memory', surfaced before long in *The Scarlet Ceremonies,* a piano work based on *The White People*. The same influence can be felt in *Legend* for piano and orchestra (dedicated to Machen) and several other compositions.

Ireland eventually reached a point where he complained about seemingly-imperceptive newspaper critics: 'How *can* they understand my music, if they've never read Machen?' Most of them never did.

It was in 1908 that the composer, nearing thirty, acknowledged that he had reached the dividing line between apprenticeship and craftsmanship by discarding, after considerable self-searching, all but a few works written before the age of twenty-one. In so doing he demonstrated the line his future musicianship was to take: quality before quantity. What he did keep, or release thereafter for publication, usually had the worth to survive fashion's vagaries.

Moeran had the following comment to make about Ireland's self-imposed ruthlessness:

'. . . when one sees a large body of works from the pen of one whose severe methods of self-criticism have suppressed all the merely experimental or imitative works (of which every musician who ever lived has had to write a fair number in his early years), one is bound to admit that its composer has made his mark in the musical world of his time.'

Generally these discarded efforts smacked of Stanford, Brahms and Dvorak, leaders of Ireland's formative years, but two of the oldest that were retained displayed a more independent mind: *Daydream* and *Meridian,* for piano. Ultimately he was talked into re-publication and, in old age, into an edition of both solos under one cover, tallying with a life-long habit of issuing piano music and songs in sets of two or three under a joint descriptive title. The publisher's initial instinct was to have them revised (as certain catalogues erroneously state was done), but Ireland stood firmly against revision to the point of obstinacy. Nor could the parties agree on the dual cover title. Arguments for and against revision ended with the composer putting his foot down once and for all. 'NO!' Ireland repeated loudly, 'how *can* a man of eighty-odd hope to get back into the mind of a boy in those days? They're young and spontaneous, and they'll have to *remain* young and spontaneous.' Like Archimedes leaping from the bath yelping 'Eureka!', John Ireland shot up from his chair with a stripling's vigour, shouting 'I've got it! *In Those Days!'*

Experienced friends differed on issuing *In Those Days.* Julian Herbage, specially close to him, expressed doubts about publishing 'juvenilia'. Sir Arthur Bliss swung to the opposite extreme. 'How old *were* you?' Bliss asked, reading the pieces through, amazed that Ireland at sixteen could achieve so much.

Each year from 1907 onwards Ireland crossed to the Channel Islands. He was a pilgrim, not one of the extrovert holiday-makers crowding the antiquated steamer with tall, sooty smokestacks. It was this journey which prompted the Weymouth guidebook for that year to remark: 'Let none consider himself a hardened salt until he has emerged scatheless from the ordeal of a rough crossing (though) to those to whom seasickness is unknown, this is a magnificent excursion.' The return fare set Ireland back a good eight shillings (40p) return, compared with the day trippers' concessionary rate of four shillings (20p).

We deliberately refer to John Ireland as a pilgrim, for it was in that spirit that he returned again and again to Jersey and to Guernsey, to revel in their prehistoric and pagan legends, ancient hill forts, grimly romantic martello towers, and air of mystery.

Towards the end of the opening decade of the present century, Ireland began reaching out towards the long creative phase of music for piano and for voice which stretched through the twenties and thirties. One should perhaps term him a setter of poems to music, and not a song-writer. Both components were equally carefully considered and married together.

Around 1912 Ireland is discovered tackling unison, two-part and choral songs; test runs for the wealth of solo songs to follow. Two may be selected as representative of these, set to a favourite poet of the cognoscenti, if not of Everyman, James Vila Blake: a *Hymn to Light,* unusual in having an organ *obbligato* part; and *Alpine Song.* The latter is melodic enough to remain staple school-choir fare, yet demonstrates the sense of space between the piano's bottom and top registers that also so gloriously characterises his best orchestral music. Who, remembering *Alpine Song* from schooldays, can forget how words and music leap up an E-flat arpeggio like a Swiss goatherd after his flock:--

> O shepherd boy, O shepherd boy!
> Thou sing'st so fresh and free,
> Upon the verdant mountainside
> Thy cheerful melody.

This up-and-coming composer was a man to watch, but he was still youthful enough to hold older composers in awe.

Though about thirty, he found himself almost tongue-tied when he met Elgar again. The occasion was one of those musical *soirées* given after dinner-parties by the aristocracy of Park Lane, though how he came to be present Ireland could not afterwards recollect. While one of Elgar's chamber works was being played Elgar himself prowled the outskirts of the assembly, constantly puffing a pipe. This pipe seemed like a conversational straw to Elgar's temporarily timid junior, thankful to grab any topic when they were afterwards brought together. 'Do you smoke while you work, Mr. Elgar?' was the only remark Ireland could think up. 'Work!' barked Elgar loudly; 'I don't understand you, Mr. Ireland!'

Another handful of organ compositions appeared in about 1911: a *Capriccio* and two pieces (*Sursum Corda, Alla Marcia*) dedicated 'to Sir Walter Parratt, MVO,' showing that Ireland as an emergent public name bore no grudge against the Parratt who had so thoughtlessly ridiculed his school-boyish boots and knickerbockers some fifteen years earlier.

In 1912 came the annual Channel Islands pilgrimage, inspiring a start on the best of all his solo piano works, rivalled but never surpassed in future years. Returning again to Jersey, alone, Ireland intended to soak up more of the prehistoric associations that so intrigued him, as well as the summer sun that beat down as he bathed one day, probably from Le Fauvic beach, half swimming and half lazing, with a mind wide open to any impression nature cared to offer. Suddenly, his best idea in months flashed upon this musician so spellbound by the island's atmosphere. Spellbound; under an island spell; even the title was handed to him at the right moment: *The Island Spell*.

Dashing straight back to his holiday bungalow on the magnificent Jerbourg Peninsula looking across to Sark and mystic Herm, he immediately put a draft onto paper. It was one of those pieces, as he said, which *had* to be written: the music was all round him, in sunlit visual form. It needed only rounding off with a final page when he returned home but Chelsea, much though he loved it, was not Jersey. An ending that felt exactly right refused to materialise, despite periodic wrestling with the partly-finished score. At the piano, his fingers never wandered into an ending leading naturally out of the other pages. After trying for several months, Ireland gave up.

Next summer, staying again at Jerbourg, bathing off the same beach in the same weather conditions, at the same hour in the selfsame month — that is, in identical circumstances — the last page flashed to mind, spontaneously and unasked.

The Island Spell was complete. It was later published, under the general heading of *Decorations* with two other pieces, *Moonglade* and *The Scarlet Ceremonies,* all three prefaced with quotations from Arthur Machen.

The Island Spell, more than any other piano composition, keeps a firm hold over pianists for its blend of sonorously exciting undertow, muted scales and arpeggios evoking both the sea and the pagan atmosphere lingering even today off the main tourist beaches, and delicate little figurations painting sunshine on the ripples of low tide. It was more than mere chance which led Ireland to use pentatonic scale figures in all three *Decorations;* a musical device believed to have been known to primitive pipers in the pagan period which he was recreating in 1912.

The Island Spell very clearly pointed Ireland out as a mature artist who had left the influences of other musicians behind. To quote Moeran again, here looking back from the early Twenties:

'... a man who, having worked hard in his youth, has decided to leave his early indiscretions on the shelf, reserving for the public eye and ear only those works in which he feels he has achieved a mature and adequate expression of his personality'.

As E J Moeran has pointed out, no composer, not even the greatest, writes masterpieces of equal stature throughout his working life. John Ireland proved fairly typical among composers in achieving an output ranging from average to extremely good, crowned by a smaller elite group of works worthy to be called masterpieces. Among these occurs the superb motet of 1912 *Many Waters Cannot Quench Love,* alternatively known as *Greater Love Hath No Man Than This.*

Greater Love was dedicated to 'Charles MacPherson Esq., and the choristers of St. Paul's Cathedral'. The writer added an orchestral part in 1924 giving the final touch of majesty which in a secular hall may appear a trifle pompous, but in its intended cathedral or greater-church setting sounds exactly right. Accoustic quality, combined with the visual dignity of the surroundings, enables this combination of choir, organ and orchestra to become in effect 'living architecture', as Boult calls music in its purest form; majestic and timeless.

Instinctively, one regrets that thirty years' work as an organist produced so little music for his favourite instrument; less than a dozen pieces, all but one — the last thing he wrote — composed for his own use.

Much more, in fact, existed — 'the finest organ music Ireland ever devised', but not one note was ever written down or published. Only his choirboys and pupils heard it, when he threw himself into the organist's traditional art of extemporisation. He extemporised in a manner none of them, reared on undistinguished Victorian fare, had encountered before. Letting fly as the congregation departed, not so much played-out of church as blasted out, he explored new registrations, subtle harmonic twists, and fascinating progressions from key to half-unrelated key, allowing the music to carry him far from the tradition his clergy considered decent and respectable. He was daring but never cruel, as certain present-day innovators are cruel to what was once melodic and harmonic order. Quite the reverse; he discovered beauty to break a sensitive listener's heart. To quote Charles Markes again: 'He could make a small boy burst into tears — his extemporisations made me weep — he produced sounds I'd never heard before.'

Indeed, this was not stuff for ecclesiastical pedants. Nor for teachers bogged down by outdated textbook thou-shalt-nots, or for those who, in later life, Ireland dubbed, with a hint of disgust, 'MusiCOLLEGEists'. New worlds opened for Charles and the other boys, after church, through the mere flattening of one note in a seemingly ordinary progression, or the then daring addition of half-discordant seconds to common — or uncommon — chords. No wonder cassocked ascetics looked askance when Ireland pulled out the stops up in the loft. His departures from hidebound tradition seemed almost heathen to them. This young Charles discovered after being allowed to take a children's service when he himself became proficient on the organ. Next day he found a note from Ireland reading: 'Charles! What on earth were you doing at the service yesterday? The Archdeacon said you were very pagan.' Charlie, who had tried to improvise in imitation of Ireland, could but answer 'Sorry, Sir; but I was only trying to play like you.' For once, his senior was reduced to an answer that was no answer: a laconic 'Oh!'

The young Ireland who seemed a 'pagan' to his straight-laced Archdeacon, and 'a tiger of a man' when he staged explosions of choirmasterly wrath to get results out of ordinary Chelsea boys and men, was not the whole Ireland, however. There was also the peacable visionary who, on Christmas Day in 1912, wrote a piece of utmost simplicity and gentleness; music cradling the Child of Bethlehem in uncomplicated yet subtle phrases which nearly seventy years of change have never rejected; the indestructible *Holy Boy*.

4. The Holy Boy

Simple to the point of austerity, *The Holy Boy* remains one of the public's favourite Ireland works, not least because it is technically easier than most of his piano music and therefore accessible to moderate amateurs; but the harmonic subtleties that sharpen the impact of the cradle-rocking motion as salt sharpens a dish are pure Ireland.

A St. Luke's chorister was the inspiration of *The Holy Boy*. To him, at least indirectly, Ireland also owed the acquisition of the house where most of his best works of maturity were composed.

Like many of life's important changes, the move from Elm Park Mansions came about casually. Always looking for fresh boys to train up against the day when his older lads' voices would break, Ireland tackled young Charles Markes: 'Have you got any school friends who'd like to join the choir?' Charles could name at least one, offhand: 'Yes, Sir; Bobby Glasby.' Bobby, son of a sculptor, lived at 14 Gunter Grove, just inland from Ireland's loved Chelsea Reach of the Thames. His father had a separate studio at the bottom of the garden wherein to hack undisturbed at his blocks of marble. The studio was in a detached building numbered 14a.

Bobby, after passing Ireland's rigorous ear, voice and sight-reading tests, duly became a chorister. He had no inkling that he would become the inspiration for *The Holy Boy*, or that as a result his face would eventually gaze down from a stained glass window in a great London church; nor that he would inspire a further Ireland work, *February's Child*, February being Bobby's natal month.

Soon after Bobby Glasby joined St. Luke's choir his father died. The studio lay undisturbed by sounds of the chisel. It was not silent for long. John Ireland realised it was the perfect place for teaching, composing, or making music with friends, and secured it for rent in about 1908, together with a small flat in the house itself. In 1915 he was able to purchase the whole four-storey house and studio in Gunter Grove, his headquarters for over forty years.

A specially happy outcome of Ireland's removal was the swift development of his friendship with a sculptor neighbour, Percy Bentham.

Percy Bentham became the closest of all John Ireland's friends in his middle years. The composer felt able to confide in him those feelings which can only be shared with those of 'equal temperament' — a fellow artist, albeit in a different branch of the arts. Moreover, Bentham was strong, active and virile, with the stamina to be an ideal walking companion; the type of man who seems to waltz through life with good fortune holding his hand, scarcely knowing a day's ill health. The shock of Bentham's tragically sudden loss in 1936 was therefore all the more severe, as can be gleaned from the heartbroken, almost bewildered letter Ireland wrote to one of his sisters:

'You will be deeply grieved to learn that my closest and dearest friend, Percy Bentham, died at 3 o'clock today (June 17th, 1936) from blood poisoning. It seems fantastic and unbelievable that such a fine constitution as his should be reduced to death in 10 days. I believe firmly the doctors killed him, as ever since he went to . . . . . Hospital and was treated by injections he has gone from bad to worse. He has been my closest and most intimate friend for 10 years, during which we have met almost daily. His character was of the purest gold. I can scarcely imagine what life will be without him. Time after time he has guided me, moderated my opinions, advised me constantly, and been a continued source of strength and affection and encouragement. It is simply inconceivable that I shall never, never see him again, or hear his cheery voice, or have before me the example of his incessant hard work and devotion to simple but true ideals. Apart from the grief and loss to his family this is the very worst thing that has ever happened in my life. That a man of blameless life, of the purest of pure hearts, of the very finest and most stable character, can be struck down and wasted in this way, causing the very bitterest grief to his relations and friends. This is indeed a problem. I shall have to think it out, somehow'

John Ireland's innate compassion, warm-heartedness and affectionate nature towards those who were fellow creatures in music and art shines so strongly through this unhappy missive that one almost counts the dead man fortunate; lucky to have had such a friend, who grieved so much at his passing.

By concentrating awhile on Ireland's first decade or so with St. Luke's, Chelsea, we can gather some illuminating insights into the composer both as a man in the company of others, and in control.

Ireland is particularly remembered from this period for two things: kindness towards those with enough musicality to be, in modern parlance, on the same wavelength; and 'a passion for nurturing talent'. These traits bear directly upon his ill-fated alliances with two women of the future, around whom posterity has woven a degree of romance despite Ireland's known suspicion of womankind — a suspicion born of a childhood domineered by three older sisters, some battle-axe landladies, a succession of griffin housekeepers, and gushing chasers after men likely to become famous. Kindness was the starting point of his brief, disastrous marriage; and his 'passion for nurturing talent' the prime reason for his involvement with the dedicatee of his great *Piano Concerto*.

Attention towards the choristers and pupils of Chelsea brought no such embarrassments down onto Ireland's head. Towards the child of one widowed mother he became almost a second father, tactfully paying half his church-school fees and giving him lessons, because the youngster's 'heaven-born' gift was too good to be lost for the sake of fees his mother could ill afford.

Charles Markes, sole survivor of Ireland's St. Luke's choir, vividly recalls how, in a famous Mendelssohn work, his impassioned boy-soprano plea, 'Oh God, hear my cry!' never reached the Almighty, nor the assembled congregation. He opened his mouth as widely as any choir trainer could wish, but no sound came out.

Ireland snatched aside the curtain which, in those days, usually hid the organist from the gaze of the faithful, as if angry at this ruination of Mendelssohn's climactic moment. Instantly anger dissolved into compassion: trembling shoulders and muffled sobs in the stalls told him that the tragedy of all cherub-voiced choirboys had overtaken Charles. In mid-phrase, his voice had broken.

Still weeping, Charles instinctively stumbled up to the loft, filled with a dreadful fear. Would he be turned out of the choir? With the gentlest compassion, his choirmaster put both arms around the sobbing boy and quietly whispered: 'Don't worry, Charlie. It's something that happens to all of us. Come to church just the same: come up and sit with me.' Ireland could, and did, throw mock or real tempers at rehearsals, to goad lethargic singers into rising above themselves, a trick of the trade used by most choirmasters. But with a broken-voiced and broken-hearted chorister, 'the tenderness of this man who could be a tiger' — Charles' own description — was something to treasure for always.

Charles thereafter sat up in the organ loft, whilst his voice decided whether to become alto, tenor or bass. He turned over the pages and marvelled at his senior's extemporisations. But Ireland had better ideas in mind for Charles, whose piano technique was developing fast under his guidance. 'I know what we'll do' he announced one day, swivelling round on the organ bench. 'We'll have you taught the organ, so you can help me. I've been wanting an assistant organist, and the Archdeacon says I may have one; and *you* are going to be that assistant. Come along, we'll have our first lesson now.' Additional organ training was given by another St. Luke's assistant organist.

Unexpectedly one day Ireland said to Charles 'You're going to play the next *Amen.*' Charles' debut as an organist was, however, a near-disaster. Over-anxious at the sudden prospect of his two-chord public performance, his concentration upon the service wavered. Into the middle of a long prayer exploded a loud premature *Amen*. Snatching the boy's hands off the manuals — too late — Ireland exclaimed 'You'll get me the sack!'

Such an organist, of course, was too valuable to be sacked on account of a pupil's lapse. He continued many more years at St. Luke's, where his choir kept a healthy respect for him. He was one of those born choirmasters or conductors who can enter almost insignificantly into a hall loud with hubbub, shouted conversation, and voices or instruments limbering up, and create instant silence without uttering a word. A 'terror' as a disciplinarian, he is said not to have been above uttering expletives in church when no congregation was present, as when the tenors in a difficult unaccompanied anthem began losing pitch, dragging down the other singers. 'Damn those tenors!' roared Ireland, glaring down from his bench. By using occasional cuss words in church, Ireland labelled himself a human being instead of a stained-glass saint — a quality his singers found singularly attractive. He who described the composer as a 'terror' and a 'tiger' at rehearsal has also called Ireland the most lovable of men.

He was human too, in showing a consistent concern about his own physical condition and harbouring a life-long dread of dentists and dentistry. Organists are not necesssarily hypocondriacs because they appear more conscious than most people of back troubles and other occupational afflictions which result from years spent in sliding up and down wooden benches.

At least one conversation is recorded on the opposing topics of health and music, featuring Ireland's perpetual lament that his old Holy Trinity organ was superior to St. Luke's. 'I'm going to be dead before I'm forty of kidney disease' moaned the organist, having roped in Charles to rub his back. While his assistant treated the offending spot, Ireland muttered condemnations against the instrument, instead of preparing himself for a hypothetical Eternity: 'This swell sounds like a pan of sausages!' or, 'Don't use the Vox Humana on tremulant; it sounds like a bleating goat!'. Ireland had a gift for graphic phraseology, as an exchange during an ill-faring choir practice demonstrates: 'Charlie! Do you think you could *contrive* to go to the piano and play the chord of C?' Tone of voice, like accentuation in music, made all the difference between ordinariness and a remark worthy of re-telling.

Ireland had an instinctive ability for putting over to a young pupil how genuine interpretation differed from mechanical performance, even in the simple matter of whether he banged, thumped, struck, diffidently tickled, or caressed a note: '*Charlie* can play C on the piano. *I* can play C on the piano. But if *Paderewski* played C on the piano . . .'

41

None rejoiced more than he when a student, disinterested in one composer, opened his heart to another, as when Charlie, after a disastrous lesson on Beethoven, with whom he felt no affinity, was switched to a Grieg dance. Ireland was so pleased that he took the Grieg copy and autographed it with a full inscription ending with 'from John Ireland'. It still exists, as a keepsake of a subsequently famous man.

Impatience, not uncommon in good teachers plagued with sometimes obtuse pupils, could evaporate like mist in sunshine into the brand of humour which those who knew Ireland always describe as 'quirky'. Again, we have a practical illustration, in a youngster making heavy weather of a piece, not helped by his teacher prowling around the room, periodically uttering an unreproducable cross between a 'Tcha', a snort and a sigh. Finally the teacher exclaimed 'Oh, get up and let *me* play!', working off his frustration on Ravel's virtuoso piano work *Gaspard de la Nuit*. At the bottom of page one he stopped and confessed, 'Well, it was dedicated to . . . . And *he* couldn't play it, either.' The quirky grin negated any hint of ill temper.

Ireland was always ready to talk about music. He would treat a boy twenty years his junior like an equal as they strolled after a lesson down to Chelsea Reach, or sat by the piano at home. When an occasion warranted, however, he could be maddeningly unforthcoming to a youngster over-full of curiosity. Unable to contain himself, after several lessons, a pupil once asked the purpose of a shapely glass carafe of colourless liquid, nearly always standing on the basement piano at Gunter Grove: 'Sir; what's that?' The one-word reply was 'Gin.'

Chelsea's more *avant-garde* citizens of the early 1900s included a woman concert pianist whose speciality was Scriabin, a composer then almost unknown in England.

Charles Markes, overhearing her practising, was as riveted by the music of Scriabin as he had been on first hearing Ireland's experiments with sevenths added to common chords. At his next lesson, bursting with excitement, he poured out a happy monologue beginning: 'On the way to school this morning, Sir, I heard some *lovely* music.' Ireland's deflating response was a monosyllabic 'Oh'. 'It was by Scriabin' persisted Charles, having seen outside the house a poster advertising the lady's forthcoming recital and having correctly put two and two together.

'You don't mean to tell me you like the music of *that* madman!' Ireland exploded.

At the Studio, between teaching and church routine, many works were wrought into shape. As the 1900s entered their teens, Ireland began the productive years which would continue until thirty years later, when deteriorating health and failing sight diminished the will and the ability to compose.

Days were already past when he had felt obliged to honour cold, ascetic churchmen in a dutiful *Te Deum,* offered in ponderous dedication to 'The Rev. ... Archdeacon of Middlesex and Rector of Chelsea.' Now a wider world was noticing John Ireland, whilst the clerics remained of only local importance.

Naturally enough, Ireland insisted upon composing privately. But choristers, pupils, friends and fellow musicians who dropped into the Studio after school, church or work to see whether he had anything new were often rewarded with the privilege of hearing, albeit incomplete, his latest idea. It might be a short song. It could be a fraction of a masterpiece, Ireland being by about 1913 engrossed in at least two things which were to bring him lasting fame: *The Forgotten Rite,* gloriously sonorous and evocative, and the song which caught the public's fancy like no other from his pen, *Sea Fever.*

When they arrived Ireland might still be incarcerated alone, battling with a phrase that refused to shape. But his piano could be clearly heard, alternately silenced and thrumming excitedly as the passage developed. At last he would emerge. Sometimes his voice and mien were as weary as if he had just chopped a hundred logs, as he muttered 'Oh, this is hard work' (a complaint repeated with much feeling a decade onwards during *Mai Dun's* birth throes). 'Ireland had an extraordinary faculty for tearing you to pieces emotionally' asserts one who often heard him playing his own music; but none is so torn physically and mentally as the artist himself, in the travail of creation. Financially there was no need to exhaust himself to achieve publication in order to earn royalties. His inheritance together with his church and teaching fees could maintain both himself and Gunter Grove. He composed for the same reason as others blessed — or cursed — with the divine spark; because he had to.

On some occasions Ireland was in the mood to relax under the influence of a good meal a good drink, and the release of a completed piece that had shaped well. Or again, the composer and his entourage of friends might troop out for a meal at a favourite haunt like the Greyfriars Restaurant, up towards Kensington, where only 1s. 3d. (about 6½p) bought repletion. Afterwards came a cheerful walk back to the Studio for more music-making.

In the summer of 1913 work began on his first important orchestral piece since the rejects of his College days, the symphonic prelude *The Forgotten Rite*. Once more Jersey and the literary influence of Machen combined to trigger off ideas; Jersey, so rich in the prehistoric aura he loved and which lured him back again and again for some thirty years.

The Forgotten Rite was the product of island impressions garnered over several stays, rather than of any particular visit or moment, though possibly the main idea took shape at Le Fauvic, birthplace of *The Island Spell*. This was Jersey off the sunbathers' tracks, where pagan mysticism lingered even into the 20th century, for those with ability to sense it. Arthur Machen's 'world beyond the walls' permeates *The Forgotten Rite's* intangible beauty; the *genius loci,* or spirit of places haunted by 'old, unhappy, far-off things'.

Once fallen in love with *The Forgotten Rite*, one can never forget it: hauntingly beautiful, fey and other-wordly. Ethereally poised, the subdued opening phrases transport the listener into other spheres of time. Ireland's hallmarks emerge as unmistakably as those on sterling silver; the dominant-ninth chord which, in its normal unoriginal form he considered vulgar, disguised into the most sensuous effects; sonorous strings; little woodwind ripples like calm Jersey wavelets; a wide sweep of orchestral grandeur, with every strand from flute down to bass separately audible. All sinks to rest at the direction *lontano posibile* (as distantly as possible), as the music melts into a faery never-never land. Ireland's list of orchestral works is short, but the best of him is in the best of them.

The Forgotten Rite's opening is among the most haunting music of our time. It haunted its own composer, subconsciously, for over forty years; the last bars he ever penned, ending a commissioned *Meditation* for organ a few years before his death, were virtually the same. Did his mind return in half-blind old age to this serenade to the Jersey he had loved since youth, or did he not realise whence came those glorious chords? We shall never know.

Four years after it was completed, *The Forgotten Rite* received its Promenade Concert premiere, in manuscript (it was not published until 1918) during a season not otherwise over-rich in works made to last. Its uneasy bedfellows ranged from Dora Bright's *Suite Bretonne for Flute and Orchestra* to a *Jolly Roger Suite* and an orchestral morsel tersely labelled *Croon.*

The Forgotten Rite is a work pervaded with veiled mystery. But the biggest mystery is its neglect except when special commemorative Ireland events bring it out to enchant new audiences. Even in his lifetime Ireland came to nickname it *Forgotten Quite.* This time his humour was not so much quirky as sad.

The year 1913 brought forth a crop of lovely songs, among them the cycle *Marigold.* Marigold is one of the plants featured in his memorial window, symbolising the flowers of which he wrote.

One song so caught singers' fancy that in its day it enjoyed the universal repetitous use of a present-day pop-song. For thousands of Uncle Bills and Cousin Roberts entertaining after tea at the parlour piano, *Sea Fever* and John Ireland were synonymous.

Once more Jersey touched off his imagination. The notorious crossing to the first outlying reefs, glimpses of the Alderney Race, and the ships' graveyards of the main islands' rockbound coasts seem to spur on each phrase of *Sea Fever* like currents under a ship's stern.

Curiously, considering Ireland's sensitivity to the rhythm of words as well as of notes, imbibed from his literary upbringing, the poet John Masefield is said to have thought rather less than the rest of the world of his setting of his verses:

I must go down to the seas again,
To the lonely sea and the sky.

45

The composer's own chief complaint was that singers usually took *Sea Fever* too fast, obscuring the luminous beauty of his unusual harmonies. More often than not his direction for a song or piano piece was not much more than an *allegretto* or some near equivalent.

Whatever the poet's or the composer's personal feelings, the public had no reservations about *Sea Fever*. Early broadcasters, discovering that its broad manly strides came better over crackling microphones than glutinous love lyrics, adopted it wholeheartedly. It was still going strong in the twenties when the BBC organised a popularity poll of all songs heard over the air, from music hall and dance band numbers upwards. *Sea Fever* effortlessly outstripped about a hundred rivals in mass opinion. The irony of this vote was not lost on the composer, who had previously seen *Sea Fever* rejected by several prominent publishers until the German publisher Augener, realising its beauty, issued it. Shortly afterwards Augener was interned. This was irresistible to Ireland's humour. His account always ran: 'A German published it eventually — and then he was interned!'

Sea Fever's popularity lasted until the era of singing around the piano was destroyed by television after the Second World War. This tragic abandonment of practical music making in favour of a box in the corner was reflected in a latter-day exchange of words between Ireland and a friend who tactlessly said, on the subject of cash, 'Oh well, *I'm* not a wealthy composer!' 'What do you mean, a wealthy composer?' retorted Ireland; 'Last year *Sea Fever* earned me only three farthings, and sold six copies.' Three farthings, pre-decimal, approximated to a quarter of a new penny.

Nonetheless, *Sea Fever* is not forgotten. One memorable phrase curves, in musical notation, across the top of Ireland's memorial window in the Church of the Holy Sepulchre, as a reminder that this was his best-known song.

Other solo- and part-songs of the immediate pre-Great War months included the attractive *Bed in Summer* and *The Echoing Green* ('To Gwennie in Jersey'. Jersey in music, yet again!). Gwennie was probably the small daughter of a local friend. Though not exactly a child-lover, Ireland had a natural affinity with children, and won their liking by treating them like intelligent adults.

The Undertone, a nostalgic piano piece, became one of a set of *Preludes* put together over four years. The others were the naturalistic *Fire of Spring; The Holy Boy,* written first but issued as No. 3; and *Obsession,* as sinister and nightmarish as its title and the wartime year (1915) of its birth.

Music's rebellion against textbook authority closely anticipated the greater rebellion of nation against nation. Composers like John Ireland questioned, as their predecessors had not dared, the colleges' inhibiting 'because-Tovey-said-so' attitude towards exploratory minds, though he accepted the truth that rules could not be overthrown until they had been assimilated: 'Before you can break them successfully, you've got to know what they are.'

It has been alleged, not without truth, that certain mammoth concertos, such as the *Tchaikovsky B-flat Minor,* are at their best when given by a performer in a temper. Strong reactions, stirred up by a world of madness, had a similar effect on wartime composers, as when Ireland began his *Second Violin Sonata* amid the turmoil of 1915. Years of death and destruction had passed already. No solution was in sight. Where would, or could, it all end?

E. J. Moeran's assessment, compiled after the war, reaches the heart of this sonata's character: 'Perhaps more than any other work belonging to the period of the Great War, it was representative of the times that produced it, and it at once revealed its composer as a man who felt deeply, even angrily, but without the sickly despondency so dangerously prevalent in those days.'

The composer himself had moments of doubt during the *Violin Sonata's* gestation, knowing in his heart that this combination of aggression and tenderness was right, but afraid that critics and audiences would find it too *avant-garde.* 'I believe I've overdone it *here'* he exclaimed one day, stabbing a finger onto a shattering passage in the manuscript. Next moment, confidence restored, he was singing the violin part to his own accompaniment in an almost rhapsodical interlude. 'You know what that is, don't you?' he remarked; 'It's a setting of a poem (here bursting into song again), "Come with me, Come to my garden".' Momentarily his song without words stilled the tumult.

Psychologically the *Sonata* was right for its time, seething with rebellion against war. Its intensity worried the composer himself when he came to play it back, alternately singing and talking as his hands crashed out explosive chords: 'Isn't this a bit much? What are they going to make of *that*?' A pianistic flurry like a salvo of shells towards an 'excruciating' climax (the composer's word) set him repeating again, 'Charlie, I'm sure I've overdone it this time!'

But Ireland had not overdone it. He saw, correctly, what ordinary people scarcely dared consider: that tumult must run its course before peace returns. The end of the slow movement, where his music climbed up from a slough of despond, pierced by unbearable beauty, towards light, told them to endure, hope, and believe. His faith in ultimate victory was affirmed in this finale, and again at the end of the second *Trio*.

Conditions at the premiere in 1917 were, like the music itself, 'psychologically right'. Both protagonists, the celebrated violinist Albert Sammons, dedicatee of the work, and the pianist William Murdoch, were in khaki army uniform, having obtained special leave for the concert. There not being much time for study and practice on active service, a younger friend naturally asked Ireland, 'How long will it take them to learn it?' 'Oh, about a fortnight. They're not like *you*, you know' he replied, with a flash of the old peacetime quirkiness.

War's ill wind blew Ireland full fame. Before the premiere of the *Second Violin Sonata* he had written his most popular song, *Sea Fever*; pianists' favourite Ireland composition, *The Island Spell*; and his loveliest orchestral essay, The *Forgotten Rite*. He had been increasingly noticed by knowledgeable musicians and critics, but was not nationally famous.

Fame burst suddenly when he was nearing the age of forty, during the 20th century's most brutal war, with this work speaking alternately of war and peace. It established him as an important composer with something to say and a highly original way of saying it, linking orderly classical form to visions of the future without overthrowing melody and harmony. Overnight recognition is rarer is reality than in fiction which features brilliant unknowns who achieve fame and love together within forty-eight newsprint-quality pages; but

48

this sonata achieved it for John Ireland. Like Lord Byron, he 'awoke next morning to find himself famous'. The publisher Winthrop Rogers was on the doorstep before breakfast, anxious to acquire it for immediate publication. The surest sign of arrival in the world of music and books is when a publisher comes to the writer, with a contract in his hand, instead of the artist having to approach several publishers. This astute gentleman had not erred in his judgement, based on one hearing, in those pre-TV days of personal music making. The entire first edition was over-subscribed before it was even printed. 'Never . . . had a chamber work by an English composer made such a sensation,' wrote a leading musicologist in retrospect.

1915 also saw the composer embarked on a sternly powerful *Rhapsody* for piano, among his most successful solo works, reflecting war's progress and yet clutching at memories of sanity. At one moment during its writing he would be toying with a simple, almost coquettish little theme; the next, building up to a terrifying climax, yelling at the top of his voice as he attacked the piano like a one-man army personally engaging with the Kaiser. 'He was a tiger of a man when he was young,' a close friend of those wartime years repeated several times during one conversation with the present author. *Rhapsody* bears him out, saying as much about its creator as his times.

The tiger could, however, calm down enough to write more music for the church. The setting in 'F' of the *Magnificat* and *Nunc Dimittis*, universally known among flippant organists as *Mag and Nunc,* dates from the same year as the *Sonata* and *Rhapsody.*

News from the trenches grew worse as the war dragged on. Those with a natural streak of humour survived best, able to cock a gibe at the Kaiser even when under threat of his most sinister visitations. Ireland, strolling back to the Studio one evening at dusk with Bobby Glasby and Charlie Markes arm-in-arm on either side, pulled up short in the wake of a gas-lamp lighter. 'Do you know what that is?' he asked as the lamplighter raised his long pole skywards. 'No, Sir' they replied (even as close friends they called him Sir long after leaving their teens). 'That's an Anti-Aircraft Zeppelin Protector' he explained, straight-faced, demonstrating how to protect themselves from a 'zepp's evil bulk by prodding it in the belly from below with a lamplighter's pole.

Presumably he looked less lightheartedly at those ugly brutes after a bomb from a zepp destroyed his treasured self-contained flat in one of Deal High Street's loveliest historic houses, a favourite peacetime refuge for thought and composition.

Little appears to have been written during 1916 except a topical but unpublished song, *A Garrison Churchyard*. During this creative lull we might therefore pause and look instead at Ireland as a person, at the approximate half-way mark of his life. Spare to the point of slightness as a young organist, he had filled out to something like the Ireland concert audiences and friends knew between the two world wars: well-covered, chubby of face as a result of his fondness for good meals followed by generous toasts in musicianly company, bright-eyed and alert, with jet black hair and 'a personality that came out and got you'. A 'complex yet simple man' according to one friend, he found no attraction in people of shallow thought, towards whom he appeared somewhat distant, but was the most loyal of friends to those with a personal affinity. A teen-aged chorister with proven ability and a sharp brain was treasured as much as an adult friend of twenty years' standing.

Sharp contrasts face every writer attempting to describe Ireland; a man uneasy in women's company who nevertheless attracted them by his distinguished physiognomy, piercing dark eyes and -- though none openly admitted it — his growing fame; one whose voice took on an icy, edgy rasp when singers ruined his music, or bawled full blast at the piano when a dogged phrase refused to go right, but was so quiet in normal use, and so gentle when people came to him in trouble; the aforesaid 'tiger' and 'terror in his cups' who confessed genuine fear of going to a dentist and worried all his life about bodily aches and pains until they were established as non-fatal; a man needing friends around him, acting the gregarious Chelsea Arts type, who periodically felt compelled to withdraw into introspection and aloneness, the mood that triggered off his most romantic or mystic music; a merciless driver as a tutor, tolerating not one wrong note, who detested practising himself.

50

Compositions of 1917 embrace three groups; chamber music, piano, and songs. The first consists of one single but important 'concoction', a one-movement *Trio* for violin, cello and piano, designed as a continuous set of variations, a comparatively daring break from stereotyped three-movement sonata-form. This *Trio,* technically Number 2, counting the *Phantasie Trio* as Number 1, 'bears the grim seal of the times' wrote Moeran. But, he continued, 'curiously enough (it) did not make the immediate impact of the *Sonata'*. After the war, however, the *Trio's* popularity picked up, and Moeran could observe: 'It is now coming into its own, as one may note from the increasing frequency of its performances.'

Despite the war, London was still London. Father Thames continued flowing through Chelsea Reach, near Ireland's home. Blackout was not rigidly observed, as in the second conflict, allowing gaslamps flickering on the Embankment still to make dust magical. The composer kept to his old habit of strolling there after teaching sessions, to freshen the minds of both master and pupils. 'Let's go for a drive' he said on impulse to Charles Markes after one evening lesson, taking his latest car, a Morgan, out to Wimbledon Common at the pace of a 'scalded cat'; a vivid memory making nonsense of the assertion that Ireland only learned to drive in the 1920s, the rights of which belong to a future chapter. Returning towards Battersea Bridge he suddenly slammed on the brakes and stopped the Morgan's careering. Pointing with a sweep of the arms towards the bridge's rows of lamps, he remarked in nursery-rhyme fashion, apparently inconsequentially, 'Twinkle, twinkle, twinkle!' Teacher and student strolled up and down the Embankment, watching inky waters pick up the reflections of the gaslamps. Thus the peacefully nocturnal *Chelsea Reach* came into being, one of the three well-known *London Pieces.* One of Ireland's first questions to Charles Markes following their post-Second World War reunion, after losing sight of one another for thirty long years was, 'Do you remember twinkle, twinkle, twinkle?'

The cheeky humour of *Ragamuffin,* Number 2 of this set, evolved out of a passing encounter in the region of St. Luke's, Chelsea. Arriving for choir practice one evening Ireland went straight into an animated description of the 'delightful' but dirty urchin he had encountered on his way, flaunting his breed's 'I care for nobody, no not I, and nobody cares for me' attitude as he jauntily whistled a perky tune. 'Something like this,' added Ireland, going to the piano and picking out the impromptu bars that became the theme of *Ragamuffin*, while its prototype mooched on his way unaware that he had just been immortalised. *Ragamuffin's* birth was among the favourite Ireland yarns of the St. Luke's choirboy turned into a famous choir trainer, Leslie Woodgate, who was present.

A third *London Piece* depicts the cosmopolitan foreign quarter, suggesting Italian street buskers in its direction *quasi tambourine*. The composer adopted a soothing old-fashioned title as alternative to the hackneyed 'morning', calling it instead *Soho Forenoons*.

If the 1917 *London Pieces* afforded a respite from war, the songs of that year underlined the reality of battle: not so much its fury as its futility and tragedy, reflected in two pairs of verses by contemporary poets.

The Cost, subtitled *Songs of a Great War*, utilised poems by E. T. Cooper; *The Cost* and *Blind*, whose tension was made almost unbearable by the music's austerity.

Rupert Brooke, before becoming a tragically young victim at the front, gave English literature two of its most memorable poems. Both were set by Ireland in 1917/18: *Blow Out, You Bugles, Blow,* and the lines most of us know by heart in their own right:

> If I should die, think only this of me:
> That there's some corner of a foreign field
> That is for ever England. . .
> *(The Soldier)*

More songs followed, including the beautiful *Spring Sorrow*. The message of its last page was the message of life itself as the struggle drew towards its close; peace will come, as spring will come again. But not yet. Its composition affords a revealing insight into the man's humility and lack of self-satisfaction. Three possible endings were under consideration, all of which he played on the piano to a pupil: one ordinary, one more original, the third having one of those twists of an unexpected accidental that make Ireland's music unmistakable. 'Which do *you* like?' he asked. '*That* one' replied the youth unhesitatingly, being unusually sensitive to quality in music. When Ireland asked him why, he replied 'Because of that flat.' The composer duly adopted this version for his poignant piano postlude beneath the long-held final word 'pain'. It is a perfect example of how one single note, illuminated by a quirk of the simplest kind, can alter the entire character of a composition from what a competent workman *might* do into what a genius *would* do.

An interesting illustration of continuity of thought was *The Sacred Flame,* on mystical Mary Coleridge verses. Its accompaniment slips at one point into a close replica of *The Forgotten Rite's* beauteous opening sequence; the phrases that recurred forty years later still as the final bars penned by the half-blind, old composer. Other settings ranged from *The Rat,* vicious as its title, to the traditional verse *I Have Twelve Oxen,* and a Christina Rossetti sequence on the subject of *Mother and Child.*

Intimate pieces displayed Ireland's awareness of the significance of keys in reflecting the temperament of a poem. 'Every key has its own colour,' he often reiterated. A-flat and G-sharp had totally different characters, though enharmonically both sprang from the same keynote. To Ireland every key, whether sharp or flat, major or minor, was as individual as one human being is from all others.

He was big-hearted enough to accept that, on occasion, a trained friend knew better than himself, being able to look more dispassionately at a manuscript. 'Why didn't you do this . . .?' enquired one of his intimates, when shown a certain song, indicating the sequence he himself felt appropriate at one point. With some surprise he questioned why the composer immediately took a pencil and altered that section. 'Why? I'm altering it because it's better,' Ireland replied.

In some piano music he looked away from international horrors, back to happy exploration of the Thames Valley at gorgeous Pangbourne (*The Towing Path*). Other examples adopted greater introspection, notably the reflective G-minor *Darkened Valley* with its *pianissimo* interlude of G-major hopefulness. Ireland's sole sonata for piano was begun in 1918. Unfortunately too difficult for any but professionals or exceptionally advanced amateurs, the *Piano Sonata* displays his command of keyboard technique as both performer and composer: complex, energetic, rugged, with a very characteristic chromatic undertow beneath the melodic mainstream.

Moeran, his contemporary and fellow-composer, wrote soon after the *Sonata's* premiere of its 'complexity of harmonic texture . . . and an elaboration which had not become developed to such a vital extent in the earlier violin sonatas and trios', and of its absolute conciseness: 'There is not a redundant note in it.' Nor did an idiom as native as Elgar's escape this analyst; if Elgar's music breathed the spirit of the Malvern Hills, Ireland's finale with its 'bold contours' epitomised 'the lofty uplands of the South Country', breathing 'the spirit of the English countryside experienced by a mind capable of the most keen human sensibility'.

Before the *Piano Sonata* was completed the Great War ended. Chelsea life and friendships resumed something of normality.

But at least one valued contact was broken, that with the choirboy grown up into a friend, Charles Markes, temporarily snapped by a combination of war and human misunderstanding.

Towards the end of the war Charles, on reaching call-up age, had enlisted. However, a fellow organ pupil and amateur violinist (with more affectation than an ear for intonation), set about securing Charles' discharge on compassionate grounds. He regarded his own well-born influence sufficient to 'wangle' a release, in view of the fact that Charles had a widowed mother.

Before the aristocrat could actually tackle the British Army single-handed to release Charlie, the Armistice decided the issue. Ireland's humour seized as joyously on this true-blue-blooded Britisher as a bird grabbing a worm. Bird, indeed, was his first nickname for the wangler, the Wangle-Wangle Bird. Before long, in the postcards and other missives leaving Gunter Grove or the church vestry in Ireland's tight, tensely 'tigerish' handwriting of youth, he was promoted higher up the social ladder as Lord Wangle of Wangle-Wangle.

Life, Charles discovered, was harsher for a demobbed serviceman returned to Civvy Street than it was before the War.

An office job, secured by Lord Wangle-Wangle, tying him to a desk until six o'clock, made attendance at choir practice almost impossible. An encounter at a party decided his future, when Markes offered to play for a singer. A professional light comedian, impressed with Charles' pianistic elan, this performer asked on the spot: 'Will you join my act?' Life on the boards was not a natural choice for a pianist whom Ireland had once wanted to send on to the great teacher Matthay (an offer refused because the pupil preferred to continue with Ireland). But it was a living, from music of some sort.

Ireland's reaction to the news that a pianist he considered brilliant intended going 'on the Halls' for monetary reasons was unexpectedly harsh. It was 'as if a curtain fell' between them. A few days later Markes encountered Ireland in the street near a famous music publisher's office. The composer, passing at only a few inches' distance, appeared to cut him dead. 'My heart broke on the spot,' Charles Markes recalled to the author.

Though distressed at the apparent end of their friendship, Markes could not abandon Ireland's music. Even an audition for the famous Co-Optimists troupe turned into a serious performance, despite the fact that Markes was expected to follow several other hopefuls in demonstrating his command of ragtime.

Knowing that ragtime was not his strong point, Markes, when his turn came, somehow found himself in a daze and playing, of all unlikely things, *The Island Spell*. When the last magical notes died away, he became conscious of people coming from backstage and across the footlights; not to shout 'What the Hell. . .' but to ask what this enchanting music was. He replied simply that it painted a picture of Jersey. Thereafter he played *The Island Spell* every night, as a contrast 'turn'. Shaking off Ireland's influence was not easy. In another Co-Optimists show he accompanied *Sea Fever* twice nightly. It always caused him a pang of regret, for a friendship destroyed in one moment. When he emigrated to Australia as musical director of the show in which he met the young dancer who became Mrs. Markes, the classical pianist turned light entertainer for a living's sake lost all sight of old times. Thirty years would elapse before a sad misunderstanding was cleared up and a perfect friendship renewed.

During those three decades another war began and ended, and Ireland composed the finest music of his maturity, a long way removed from the gentle simplicity of *The Holy Boy*.

5. Mai-Dun

Screaming and whirling a primitive sling, the man, naked but for a goatskin loin cloth, ran to join the throng fighting around the main entry to a huge Wessex earthwork. This battling human mass comprised courageous but disorganised native Britons and ruthlessly disciplined Romans. Next moment he uttered a long death screech. His ammunition of Dorset beach stones fell uselessly as he dropped among the fallen.

In a Dorchester museum he still lies exactly as he fell, about eighteen centuries ago, with a vicious Roman arrow-head of iron wedged between two vertebrae, hacking his spine apart as neatly as a pig's back in a modern butchery. He was one of scores slain that day in AD 43 on the ramparts now called Maiden Castle, slaughtered by Vespasian's legions. Though well guarded near the entrance, the vast hillock was ill-protected elsewhere. Roman soldiers advanced quickly towards local women and children huddled inside primitive huts within a central reservation, spearing the defenders as they went. Conquest was not tempered with mercy; maddened by the resistance, the Romans burned the huts, murdered their inmates, killed any remaining defenders, and flung them irreverently into trenches before marching off to their next objective.

Guidebook writers do their best to reconstruct this bloodiest of ancient battles. Thomas Hardy, semi-fictionalising Maiden Castle into Mai-Dun, did considerably better. But neither could reproduce the actual noise of voices and weapons.

Today two methods exist for recreating such a scene in sound: use of recorded effects for television and the cinema, or more imaginative sound painting by means of a full modern orchestra. John Ireland chose the orchestra and, like Vespasian's legions, won hands down.

In *Mai-Dun,* described as a *Symphonic Rhapsody,* he achieved a landmark work at the outset of the twenties. It saw him acting as a musical H G Wells, looking forward and backward at the same moment: backward to a battle whose extent was scarcely guessed at by historians when he began writing the rhapsody, and forward to Sir Mortimer Wheeler's gruesome archaeological confirmation of the manner in which Maiden Castle and its defenders fell, which did not come until about seventeen years after *Mai-Dun's* concert premiere.

A searing orchestral spear-thrust sets the scene in one savage stroke. Furiously, battle is engaged until Ireland's instinct for unashamedly lyrical melody asserts itself. A lull in the music suggests the resignation of the women and the nobility of the defence offered by the outnumbered men. The resumed struggle obliterates this brief peace. Weapons seem to clash against shields, stones to whizz from slings, in a clatter of percussion. Piercing trumpet calls spur the legions on to the kill, achieved in a blazing coda marked 'fff'; louder than the loudest.

A former horn player of the Bournemouth Symphony Orchestra perfectly demonstrated how this music could bring distant history alive when he stressed the benefit of knowing *Mai-Dun* from actual performance *before* visiting the castle itself. Warring Britons and Roman soldiers immediately came to his mind's eye on viewing the empty green ramparts, simply from his acquaintanceship with Ireland's music.

An old Chelsea colleague said of Ireland: 'he wrote music with his own blood', if a poem, book, picture or place virtually compelled him to translate it into sound. Philip Heseltine (Peter Warlock) waxed more bitter in updating the old maxim, 'talent does what it *can*; genius does what it *must,* into 'genius is undervalued, while mere talent is overpraised'. But, in fairness, the world found no praise too high for works standing out above general mediocrity. To quote Moeran again, in 1923: 'The culminating point up to the present of Ireland's maturity is to be found in the *Symphonic Rhapsody (Mai-Dun)* for orchestra . . . the work of a man whose spiritual outlook is engirt, so to speak, with the influences engendered by nature, susceptible to the irony as well as the beauties of existence'; a man finding Machen's 'world beyond the walls' in the atmosphere of Maiden Castle.

To alter one phrase of *Mai-Dun* might appear impossible, so tightly knit is the whole. This was Elgar's first reaction when *Mai-Dun*, unpublished and still in manuscript, appeared on the same Queen's Hall programme as one of the older master's compositions. 'That is a very fine work of yours' declared Elgar, handing Ireland his visiting card. 'Bring it along to my address tomorrow morning; I'd like to go through the manuscript with you.'

Next morning the two composers went through *Mai-Dun* together, page by page. 'Splendid!' exclaimed Elgar, 'I wouldn't alter a note of it', and then went straight on to explain to Ireland exactly how he *would* alter it, to even better effect. They discussed orchestration in particular (the best lesson in the subject he ever had, Ireland reiterated to the end of his days), and the particular benefit of studying Liszt's then fashionable orchestral poems, whose opulence was not unlike that of Ireland and Elgar in their most expansive melodic moods. Elgar's cordiality and encouragement were never forgotten. Professional jealousy had no place when the creator of *Gerontius* confessed how much *Mai-Dun* had impressed him.

In later years Ireland became increasingly sensitive to real or imagined neglect of his music, in a world which had turned its back on emotion in favour of arid unmelodious note-patterns. The irony that dubbed *The Forgotten Rite* as *Forgotten Quite* turned *Mai-Dun* into *May Not Be Done* as its novelty wore off on concert promoters. Asked during his declining years whether he was free to accept a Promenade concert commission for a new work — proof that, in fact, Ireland was *not* forgotten — his reply to the BBC was 'Well, you can have *Forgotten Quite* and *May Not Be Done*, which I think can be counted as new works.' In any case, rapidly failing sight would have precluded acceptance of the invitation at that late stage. On one occasion Ireland turned the tables on himself with unintentionally comic effect. During a discussion at the BBC the usual complaint of neglect wormed its way into the conversation. 'Oh, come off it, John!' retorted his lifelong broadcaster friend, Julian Herbage; 'Barbirolli is playing your *Mai-Dun* this week, and the *Concertino Pastorale* is also being broadcast.' Ireland immediately sprang to defend *May Not Be Done* against excessive exposure, with the usual gloriously laconic Oh!; 'Oh! Now I suppose they want to *kill* my music by over-playing it!'

One wonders what Ireland would say today, on seeing Maiden Castle's ramparts in stained glass, to remind us all that *Mai-Dun,* neither neglected nor over-played, is among his greatest legacies to twentieth century music.

In the year of *Mai-Dun* he rediscovered the undulating Sussex loveliness he first sampled as a choristers' holiday leader at Worthing, through driving up to the lovely Chanctonbury Ring viewpoint with another old friend, the critic and reviewer Christopher a Becket Williams. Journalists writing up this particular topographical 'love affair' sometimes fall into the trap of assuming that, because Becket Williams guided Ireland with a running commentary on driving the car, Ireland was a learner. As previously pointed out, he bought a rakish Rex motorcycle at a very early date, and acquired a car in which to drive 'like a scalded cat' around a largely live-horse-powered London, directly his inheritance became his own. At only thirteen, we recall, he was able to cover a day-long return trip from Manchester to London, including time for an audition, because his parents were so accustomed to his spending entire days at an early motor show as to assume he was there again. Ireland, therefore, was no novice, but a prospective buyer of Becket Williams' Morgan three-wheeler, taking a Sussex test-run. The composer, disliking the car and strong willed enough to resist eloquent sales-talk, declined to make out a cheque; but he did not feel that the afternoon was wasted. He had rejected an unsuitable car, but discovered that yet another corner of Britain had power to draw him magnetically to itself: the countryside running inland from between Worthing and Shoreham-by-Sea towards Steyning and the hills culminating in Chanctonbury Ring.

It was inevitable that this new love would quickly bring forth what the Bible termed 'musical tunes', and songs founded upon 'verses in writing'.

Captivated by these breezy pea-green uplands and the enchanting villages huddled beneath them, Ireland took permanent lodgings at Ashington, looking directly towards Chanctonbury Ring. It was the first step towards his abandonment of an increasingly noisy Chelsea, thirty-three years later.

The next object of his motoring affections, acquired instead of the three-wheeler, was a Talbot Ten. He came to love it almost like a living thing, his favourite car. In later years he frequently drove down from Chelsea for weekends at The Old Rectory in which he rented a wing converted into a self-contained flat, where a devoted 'Nannie' cooked his meals. London uproar, left behind, was replaced by the sounds of birds and the chirruping of any early-rising Sussex cat that had a cheery 'purrow' in response to a tickle behind the ears.

Many ideas sprang from morning strolls, exploratory drives, or climbs up to the ancient tumuli and barrows scattering the downlands, appealing to his lifelong affinity with pre-history. Mystery and the mystic drew him as strongly here as in the Channel Islands, within far closer reach of the Chelsea studio where they took written shape.

Mai-Dun and some chamber music apart, Ireland concentrated during the twenties on songs and piano music. They have aptly been called his 'personal biography', reflecting his current literary and musical tastes. His style had matured into a very individual idiom, based on that idiosyncratic command of harmonies designed to puzzle, soothe and intrigue the ear at one and the same time. It did not alter much afterwards, except to become more concentrated and assured.

A story is told of Ireland, as organist of St. Luke's, Chelsea, walking along the upper gallery to the music cupboard in search of a suitable voluntary, pursued by a choirboy who grabbed his coat saying: 'No! Please, Sir, give us some *real* music,' meaning Ireland extemporisations instead of academic Bach. The songs and piano pieces of the Twenties were of the same stuff; *real* music, saying in a few compact pages all that need be said of a tree, flower, place, or train of thought.

The Land of Lost Content, in the then popular song-cycle form, utilised six poems from Housman's immortal *A Shropshire Lad*; yearning, bitter-sweet and expressive. More personal was a version of the traditional *Cadet Roussel,* written in harness with Frank Bridge, Eugene Goossens and Arnold Bax, each setting the same words in his own manner.

On a Birthday Morning, inscribed 'Pro Amicitia, Feb 22, 1922' ('for friendship . . .') began a chain of piano items and songs all dedicated to one friend. Almost every year during the twenties a new birthday present appeared, inscribed simply 'To AGM for Feb. 22.' They included *Love and Friendship, Bergomask, When I am Dead, My Dearest,* the song cycle, *We'll to the Woods No More,* and *February's Child,* dedicated to AGM but inspired by Bobby Glasby — the Holy Boy — whose own birthday was in February.

Who was the elusive AGM or Arthur? When Ireland first knew him Arthur G Miller, to identify him fully, was a St. Luke's chorister, the small son of a Chelsea antique dealer. As proprietors of Miller's of Chelsea, in the now touristic Kings Road, the boy's family became good friends of the musician, who acquired some of his favourite antique pieces from their shop. These were with him, in Sussex, to the end.

Ireland, despite technical complexity in his writing, preferred simplicity in actual titles. Rarely in his piano solos did they exceed three words. *Two Pieces* of 1921 illustrate both points: *For Remembrance* (literally bitter-sweet; sweetly flowing but with astringent chromatic counter-currents descending beneath its upper melody), and *Amberley Wild Brooks.*

Amberley Wild Brooks portrays a favourite spot in Sussex, where tributaries meet a widening river as it flows in looping meanders towards the South Coast. Here Ireland regularly pulled-in his car to sit, at the wheel, gazing across peaceful water-meadows. Thus, two musical lines again run concurrently; delicate upward ripples of water touching bed-rocks or bankside growth, and stronger left-hand arpeggios like a wider tide. The whole spirit of pastoral Sussex is in these six printed pages. A painting commissioned from the modern artist Juliet Pannett for the sleeve of a new record including *Amberley Wild Brooks* shows the identical view today, virtually unchanged. It is one of a trio from the same painter, the others — corresponding to different phases in his career as a writer for piano — illustrate Chelsea Reach, based on a

62

late 19th century photograph by a friend of Whistler, and Le Catioroc in Guernsey, from the spot where Ireland habitually sat in his car watching the sun sink over lonely Lihou island.

Amberley illustrates his capacity for putting complete scenes into music, but he responded equally to smaller aspects of nature; a single flower or tree. Glancing momentarily back to about 1913 affords an excellent example of the latter, *The Almond Tree*. Not trees, plural, but one specific tree. It was not even real, but seen in the window of a Chelsea art shop one Sunday as he strolled home after playing Evensong, shown in an exquisite Japanese print featuring one of the East's most characteristic blossoming trees against an almost luminous blue sky. Ireland, captivated, would have bought it on the spot, had the shop not been closed for the weekend. Next morning he hurried back to the shop, but someone else had beaten him by a few minutes. The picture was sold. His brief enchantment and its dissolution into disappointment both went into *The Almond Tree*. 'I *wish* I'd been able to get that print,' he often said wistfully in old age: 'It was *so* lovely.'

Again in Sussex, Ireland is seen drinking in the exhilaration of high winds on a favourite Downland summit. Some dislike being buffeted, and treated like human scrap-paper, but Ireland revelled in the power of unseen forces. Instead of irritating him and sending him home with his coat collar turned up, this gale of 1922 excited him. As Elgar, in *Gerontius,* caught a 'summer wind among the lofty pines' so Ireland translated this Sussex equinoctial gale into piano notation. *Equinox,* a dazzlingly difficult concert study, needs a superb executant to make its effect; one with monumental technique and imagination to feel nature in every sweep up the keyboard.

1923 brought Ireland formally back to the Royal College of Music as a professor, almost exactly thirty years after he entered its portals as a knickerbockered stripling set on becoming a concert pianist.

As a College tutor, dealing with earnest young men and girls of high ambition and corresponding incentive, he was even more successful than with ordinary men and boys at church, equipped with voices but generally of no special talent. The list of his most famous ex-pupils reads like a composers' *Who's Who*: Benjamin Britten, Alan Bush, Humphrey Searle, E J Moeran, and Richard Arnell. For many years he proved himself an outstanding teacher, examiner and lecturer, skills which are not automatically present in men of high creative ability.

A year after becoming a College professor, Ireland was made Honorary RCM, a tribute quickly repeated by the rival Academy. The only fly of contention in the ointment of creative success and increasing income from royalties and teaching was the objection of the College's governors to his preference for having students to his own Chelsea studio instead of always using College accommodation.

These students, together with private composition pupils, beat a well-worn path to 14 Gunter Grove, and down the garden to 14a, the studio. Availability of his own gramophone and records for demonstration purposes, plus freedom to give trainees more time than in an institution where practice rooms must be vacated to make way for others, were his prime reasons for teaching Royal College students, where possible, out at Chelsea. For a long time the College frowned on this departure without actually banning it, but when Sir Hugh Allen became Principal the system was stopped. It was 'not customary', and Sir Hugh did not approve. This, of course, applied to official College students, and not to private pupils, who attended the studio as usual.

Allen's successors long ago foregave Ireland his stand against formality. His old room at the College is now named the Ireland Room.

As a tutor Ireland was noted for the 'passion for nurturing talent', and eternal searching for unusual ability, which had distinguished him from the normal run of church choirmasters. The contradictions in his character were still as marked. His voice cut like a primed razor-blade when in sarcastic 'tiger' mood, or when an obtuse youngster missed the inner message of his or anyone else's music, but became so sympathetic on other occasions that few hesitated to confide in him when in trouble — a factor responsible for his short-lived marriage.

Far beyond their College years, students remembered his

kindness and encouragement. 'Now look, my boy, you're good' he addressed one sixteen-year-old pianist suffering acute depression after being reminded that an English upbringing hindered native musicians hoping for a career; 'Don't you take any notice of those Jeremiahs; you'll get there.' The lad, who had played Mozart for Ireland and therefore was in no way favoured for specialising in his teacher's compositions, did 'get there'. Bryan Vickers, the student who made good, never forgot Ireland's encouragement in his darkest hour of doubt. Another ex-College student confirmed this generous warmth of heart, enshrined in the short notes in small neat script which his tutor tended to scatter among friends and pupils with prodigality. 'Sometimes when I get depressed,' he confessed, 'I take out a little pack of letters. They're full of encouragement, and I feel better after I've read them.' Sir Arthur Bliss, too, kept by him a stack of Ireland's letters of encouragement.

Generous; kind; lovable; contradictory and paradoxical; that was the Ireland of College days. A man called a tiger, yet termed lovable in almost the same breath; one uneasy in female company who, perversely, exerted a strong attraction on girl students, for a reason as old as Eve: that a man who takes little notice of an attractive woman is more intriguing than one who does. One or two were not above going all-out to catch his eye. An illustration of this is still handed down gleefully to those likely to appreciate a tale of tit for tat. The girl, when Ireland's friends came to meet her later, was still attractive. As a student she was probably a beauty, but her crush on the composer was a distinctly one-sided business. Ireland seemed aware only of how well, or how badly, she played. She would *make* the composer notice her. An entire quarter's dress allowance from her parents was accordingly spent in a Bond Street milliner's shop on a hat to end all hats. Donning it next day, she marched up to the studio for her lesson, but her teacher appeared totally oblivious to the fashion plate on the piano stool. 'Well, Miss . . . . . the time has come for us to part' he said, bringing the session to a formal end. Still no mention of the hat. At last Ireland held out his hand, looked at her, staged a sham start of surprise and remarked 'Oh! Going to a wedding?'

Old pupils had a habit of becoming personal friends and confidantes of future days, as did Charles Markes and Bobby Glasby from St. Luke's. Percy Turnbull was a further example; loyal through another war and into Ireland's declining period.

Turnbull was a thoroughly sympathetic interpreter of Ireland's piano repertoire, possessed of the keyboard competence that is essential when complexity should appear second to an inner message. Both men firmly believed in the basic truth of interpretation; that music is perfectly capable of speaking for itself, without the antics of the showier type of concert pianist. The object was to breathe back into a page of Ireland the life enshrined there. No less. And no more. Ireland valued men like Percy Turnbull for their modesty; such modesty that the latter even disliked having holiday photographs taken when spending happy hours with Ireland and another friend, John Longmire, in Guernsey.

Most important among Ireland's compositions of the mid-Twenties was his solitary *Cello Sonata*, suggested in part by the Devil's Jumps on the legend-soaked Sussex Downs. After Elgar's lovely concerto for this eloquent instrument, a good modern but melodic sonata was sorely needed as a musical blood transfusion into the cello's pathetically limited repertory.

Ireland's *Sonata* counted among his best abstract music-for-music's-sake compositions. The Spaniard Antoni Sala first gave this very English sonata publicly, having flown here specially from Spain to record it for Columbia, with the composer at the piano. Ireland's music, incidentally, has long been popular in Spain and in New Mexico. Casals, who wrote in glowing terms of this *Sonata* to Ralph Hill, had every intention of playing it himself during a visit to England. Unfortunately, political upheavals prevented what would have been an outstanding concert. Conflicting emotions flit across the *Cello Sonata*, like the sun and cloud lighting his programmatic pictures. It embraces ecstasy and despair, Paradise and Hades, tranquillity and terror, absorbed from a passing preoccupation with Blake's *Heaven and Hell.*

Analysing Ireland's technique when the *Cello Sonata* was in its final stages of preparation, another pupil turned both friend and critic, E J Moeran, summed up thus:

'A casual glance at a characteristic page of Ireland's work might lead one to think that his chief strength lay in the richness and variety of his harmonic texture. But harmonic texture without line and form is like flesh without a skeleton; and yet so rarely is complete mastery in these respects to be observed in any composer's work, that at first glance Ireland's harmonic elaboration is a little baffling. For it is not enough to grasp merely the big lines of a work of his. Every bar, every note, has its precise significance in relation to the whole ... the argument never flags in this music; it is concise and reasoned, and there is neither repetition for formality's sake, nor redundant padding and perfunctory working-out. It is this meticulous attention to detail, and a spacious vision in which the whole work is continually held throughout the progress of its composition, that allows Ireland to succeed equally well as a writer in small and extended form,'

While *Sea Fever* and the *Violin Sonata* caught the public imagination, it was *Mai-Dun* and the *Cello Sonata* which set professional critics speculating on what might appear next to enhance Ireland's growing reputation. They had not long to wait. In 1924 he brought off another triumph — not a large-scale work such as an opera or a symphony which a generation nurtured in the belief that biggest was automatically best might reasonably have expected, but a hymn tune which occupied barely a quarter of the average sheet of music manuscript paper. It was a quixotic gesture, typical of the man. This hymn has ever since exerted such a universal and powerful appeal that multitudes of those who would not otherwise know his name are familiar with one aspect, at least, of Ireland's distinctive genius.

This miniature, destined to survive while the operas and oratorios of other composers slid into obscurity after one performance, was an eight-line setting of 17th century verses beginning:

> My song is love unknown,
> My Saviour's love to me;
> Love to the loveless shown,
> That they might lovely be.
> O, who am I
> That for my sake
> My Lord should take
> Frail flesh, and die?

Long since, several older tunes for these words have been jettisoned by common consent of clergy, choristers and congregations, leaving *Love Unknown* as irrevocably married to them as Wesley's immortal tune *Aurelia* is to 'The Church's one Foundation'.

Love Unknown was composed during a lunch with Geoffrey Shaw, co-editor with Ralph Vaughan Williams of the forthcoming *English Hymnal*. About halfway through their meal Shaw handed his guest a slip of paper, saying 'I want a tune for this lovely poem of Samuel Crossman.' The composer took the paper, read the verses through several times, took out a pencil and picked up the menu. After writing on the back of the menu for a few minutes he handed it to Shaw, with the casual remark: 'Here is your tune.' Thus was born *Love Unknown* which, a few years ago, was voted the most popular of all hymn melodies of any period.

Love Unknown was not quite what churchgoers and organists of 1924 expected of a new hymn tune, with its alternating six- and four-note bars and the unexpected chromatic note halfway through which brands it as Ireland's handiwork. Ninety-nine English hymn writers would probably have used the undistinguished sequence B-flat, D, C, B-flat at the words 'O, who am I?': Ireland flattened the D instinctively, lifting *Love Unknown* out of the rut of competence inhabited by thousands of workmanlike tunes, most of which are lost when the plough of a revised-version hymnal runs over them; 'That flat,' to use again Charles Markes' definition of the one note making all the difference to an Ireland phrase.

Chelsea, a companion hymn tune beginning with the same notes as the opening of *Chelsea Reach,* follows our 300-year-old national tradition of naming hymns after places associated with their composers. So far it has not found the same favour as *Love Unknown*. Requests for permission to reproduce the latter in new hymnals continue flowing in from countries as diverse as the United States, Japan, Hong Kong, Canada and Australasia.

An immediate result of Ireland's 1920 visit to Hardy's Dorset, centred on Maiden Castle, was *Mai-Dun*. A few years later he turned intensively to Hardy in his poetical capacity, setting *Great Things* and two cycles of related songs. Childhood immersion in poetry and everyday contact with poets ensured a special delicacy and understanding in matching word tones with musical sounds, or with subtle accompaniment details, and in devising piano preludes and postludes far removed from the brash 'casting-on' passages of Edwardian ballads, thumped by heavy-fisted amateurs out of cowering parlour uprights. Ideally, Hardy and Ireland in harness needed accompanists, who, though discreet, knew when not to understate some telling detail referring directly to the text. Five further Hardy settings pulled Ireland in two directions; richly inventive of harmony, yet incorporating prophetically astringent forecasts of the atonality which many modern composers adopted to excessively dry effect, instead of using it sparingly to create a particular atmospheric impression.

As self-contradictory in music as in life, Ireland in 1926 began a *Sonatina* for piano, whose construction harked back to the uncluttered outline of Mozart's and Beethoven's miniature sonatas under the same title, but whose emotional content departed far from tightly-reined academic orthodoxy. Described as frenzied and nightmarish, the temperamental upheavals of Ireland's *Sonatina* are obvious to the most casual listener. Better hidden is the secondary idea which a novelist would term the sub-plot. This, one of Ireland's cleverest turns of wry humour, derives from just three notes, almost too short to be termed a theme.

Those three notes preserve for posterity an otherwise forgotten and ephemeral incident between two famous composers whose relationship, though long-lasting, had a tendency at times to become an armed friendship.

As with most good anecdotes, this has acquired alternative versions in the retelling. One makes the wronged heroine a lady friend of Ireland's whose attention was filched by Arnold Bax. Another, reasonably, if less romantically, calls her a friend whom Ireland, rightly or wrongly, considered had been treated badly by Bax. On her behalf Ireland took up cudgels in a manner only a musician could have dreamed up, by enshrining his temporarily lowered opinion of the 'villain' within the composition he chanced to have on hand, the *Sonatina*. The central argument of one page thus comprises various treatments of a repetitive theme on the notes C, A, and D, spelling out the twenties' popular alternative term for a bounder, 'CAD'.

Time healed this, as it does most tiffs between close colleagues. Bax the cad reverted into Bax the old friend.

A more immediate hazard to Ireland than a fellow composer bent on revenge, after being labelled a cad for life, was a less distinguished citizen than Bax; that faceless universal threatener calling himself Anonymous. All Ireland knew of Anon was his seemingly genuine abhorrence of modern music, seething off the crumpled face of a grubby note shoved untidily through the Gunter Grove letterbox after a public performance of the piano *Sonatina,* reading' 'If you write any more music like that I shall SHOOT YOU!'

Instead of becoming a corpse on one of those lurid newspaper placards that delight in deaths of famous men, he survived this nameless threat, as he survived the tumultuous period whose overtones crept into his music, and did fleetingly put him into London's headlines. This was his brief and disastrous excursion into matrimony during 1927.

As has already been pointed out, Ireland exerted a certain attraction upon girl students, partly based on womens' traditional perverseness in setting sights on men who were noticeably uneasy in their company, and partly on the lure of fame. From babyhood Ireland had suffered excessive female domination. Three elder sisters, naturally enough, exerted the teenager's instinct to sit upon a younger brother, or mete out such punishments as lonely incarceration in his room for the petty pecadilloes his ailing mother missed. Then followed a succession of London landladies, gimlet-eyed for students' thoughtless failings. As a bachelor professor with a four-storey house, his aversion was not diminished by housekeepers ranging from pleasantly competent ladies down to a griffin in forbidding black before whom he preferred not to exchange one word with visitors, exhorting them to clam-like silence until 'She' had departed with her tea tray.

The handful of intimates knowing of his sudden marriage at the age of 48 to a gifted student of about sixteen could envisage no outcome other than catastrophe.

Again, more than one version of the episode's origins exists, though its development and abrupt ending are clear. One close friend pictures the girl, Dorothy Phillips, as being removed in this mercurially chivalrous manner from the persistent unwanted attentions of another RCM professor. The composer's own outline was recounted to the writer by a close companion of his maturer years as 'another of his quixotic acts', attributed to the same kindness towards talent in trouble that had made him act like a second father to a choirboy lacking the price of piano lessons.

Quixotic was an appropriate word for Ireland's marriage with this girl some thirty years his junior; incautious, rash, foolhardy, impetuous and precipitate. In hackneyed but time-tested terms, it was a classic case of 'Marry in haste, repent at leisure.'

Dorothy Phillips — Dophie to student friends — was not up to standard one day at her private lesson in Gunter Grove. Her playing had for some time been deteriorating, a fact not unnoticed by her tutor. Instead of attributing an uncharacteristically shoddy performance to laziness, or neglect of practice in favour of other pursuits, Ireland probed into the problem, suspecting that some larger trouble was behind this lapse in a girl he considered, in his own words, 'very promising'.

'You're obviously not playing at your best. May I ask if there's anything on your mind which I can help you over?' he enquired outright, in so kindly a manner that the girl burst into tears as he sat by her at the piano. She launched into a tirade against an apparently overbearing father couched, even in distress, in more formal language than anyone would use today: 'I'm very unhappy at home. Father is so unkind and doesn't understand me at all. Is there anything you can do to intervene with my father?'

'I'm only your music teacher, and wouldn't want to come between you and your parents,' Ireland stalled.

'*You're* my master!' she sobbed dramatically, with a hint of the twenties film heroine in her histrionics. But, mindful of the perils of meddling in family affairs, he repeated quite correctly: 'I *am* your master,' meaning her music master, 'but that doesn't give me any right to interfere between father and daughter.'

Nevertheless, after Dorothy Phillips had left Gunter Grove, her trainer turned the problem over again in his mind until a startling answer presented itself. As he recalled, 'Then the *Devil* told me what I could do. That was, to give her my name, as Mrs. Ireland. I'd be her legal protector. No-one would have any legal control over her.'

'The only thing I can do is to go through a form of marriage with you' was therefore the solution he offered next time she came, a headstrong variation on the timeless proposal, 'Let me take you away from all this,' made without full consideration of its long term implications. She jumped at the suggestion.

Briefly the register office marriage featured on London's newspaper placards, but 'Well-known composer weds' caused only a knowledgeable handful actually to speculate 'I wonder whether that's John Ireland?' The great multitude were more interested in dance-band leaders and music hall stars than classical musicians.

That this incongruous pairing was a calamity became apparent within hours. The union was never consummated. Next day, wearing the haggard appearance of a man who has wrestled half the night with the realisation that he has been trapped, he admitted outright to one of the few in the know that the venture was 'all a ghastly mistake'. His answer to another's puzzled enquiry, 'Why *did* you get married?' expressed some time afterwards, was much the same, barked out in the edgy, irritated tone of one tried to his limits: 'I must have been MAD!'

The new Mrs. Ireland's reign was short and stormy. Young and full of vitality, talented but self-willed, she soon became dissatisfied with being a composer's wife. Married only in name, she made no secret of her disappointment at the trend her visions of homelike security were taking, venting her frustration in bitterness and extravagance.

For this ill-matched pair there could be only one logical step. The marriage was annulled.

Ireland never, so far as we know, broached the subject of matrimony to another woman. He rarely mentioned this traumatic experiment even to his nearest comrades. He returned thankfully to his original status, and always insisted that

Who's Who should describe him as a bachelor. He was administered to by a further series of housekeepers ranging from overbearing to tolerable until chance presented him with an ideal solution when he was sick and abandoned by the most heartless of them, some sixteen years later.

Significantly, virtually nothing on the long list of Ireland's works bears the composition date of 1928, the aftermath year of his marriage, but by 1929 his old sense of humour and creative urge reasserted themselves. Work began on the agitated *Ballade* for piano, no relation to the lesser *Ballade of London Nights,* published posthumously and lacking the sheer genius of the 1929 work. A major song cycle was also begun, *Songs Sacred and Profane,* which occupied him, off and on, for two years. These songs ran the full gamut of life and emotion, from the gentle birth of Christ, via two aspects of secular love, to a diabolical touch in *The Soldier's Return* and ironical humour in *The Scapegoat.* Those who heard Ireland himself accompany a performance at Wigmore Hall, during the 1951 Festival of Britain, did not easily forget the manner in which he set one of the staidest musical companies in London laughing aloud as the Scapegoat's figuration skipped in company with the words 'Dances on, and on, and on!' up the keyboard. Inciting an 'excessively sober' Wigmore Hall audience with such a quizzically impish grin from the stage was, in thirties parlance, just not done. But Ireland did it, and for once the Wigmore echoed to delighted laughter.

A man who could make such a difficult audience chuckle was temperamentally better equipped than many serious artists to face up to the prospect of another world war, as the news from Europe became more worrying.

6. Green Ways

'Make hay while the sun shines' could have been the motto of
the 1930s before the advent of another headlong rush towards
war; an era of coming-out parties and tea dances, when every
suburb had its live Hippodrome or Empire, and nine old
pence (just under 4p) bought two best stalls at the black-and-
white 'flicks' for an engaged couple, plus a large bagful of
coconut ice.

Ireland, a born wit and humourist despite the solemnity of
his calling, was thoroughly at home in this decade. Though
no longer regarded as being in first youth, which counted
anything from acceptance by a publisher to the birthday of
an acquaintance's cat an occasion for Gunter Arms celebration, he was as convivial as any twenty-year-old when in
gregarious mood, and infinitely more witty. Tone of voice,
facial expression and natural comedy acting explained why
other men colliding with London street furniture were totally
unmemorable, whereas Ireland apologising in Chaplinesque
vein to a lamp-post with the wry joke, 'I shouldn't be like
this after only ten Johnnie Walkers!' is still hilarious in the re-
telling. In retired old age it was Chelsea life that reduced him
to greatest nostalgia, as in this tribute to a recently departed
old crony in a letter of 1955: 'I remember him at a sort of
tea-party in Chelsea where there was a "soda-water fight" —
one of the diversions in those carefree days!'

Ireland, between settling in Chelsea in 1908 and leaving it
in 1953, made as many friends as his character had sides:
church choristers and ex-pupils; organists and examiners;
school teachers and scholars; sculptors and painters; publi-
cans, if not sinners. Friendships were as important as music,
though each person was kept in such a watertight compart-
ment, made to feel through Ireland's prolific letter-writing as

though he were the only one, that to this day some of his closest friends scarcely know each other. All agree on one point, however, that Ireland was fun.

'He could have been another George Robey,' summed up Mrs. Marjorie Walde, recalling how the composer's friendship with her husband, the Rev. Paul Walde, spanned some fifty years from their days together as curate and organist at St. Luke's, Chelsea; 'he was so funny you could forgive him anything; he just said what was in his mind without any thought of giving offence'.

Ireland even looked like the famous comedian when he wore a certain hat, as a correspondent from Canada pointed out when relating one of his unrehearsed acts of whimsical humour:

> 'Sometime in the middle 20s I went to a concert at the Albert Hall and heard Strauss' *Alpine Symphony* and *Festal Prelude* conducted by their composer. Afterwards I fetched up with Ireland (I was a pupil of his at the time). As we passed the bust of Sir Joseph Barnby, Ireland stopped, took off his hat (a bowler — people said it made him look like George Robey) and bowed low before it; not a word was spoken and we passed on our way.'

He always raised his hat, Robey fashion, when driven past the RCM, or past Vaughan Williams' 'little house on the Embankment', as V.W. described it when he first lived there.

A humourist whose tongue could turn from caustic comment to wry drollery in seconds; a marvellous mimic; unashamedly fond of good food and wine in plenty, and unconcerned for the consequent expansion of his formerly spare frame and single chin; a hilarious companion when not withdrawn into a composition that would not go right; still something of a Bohemian; a character — and a genius. That was Ireland as the twenties merged into the thirties.

This was the same Ireland who, when war broke out again, could still mention undarned socks and unwashed underwear on the same page of a letter as the travails of composing a major work of music; the Ireland over whose 'funny little ways' friends chuckled reminiscently with the present writer as joyously as though an incident had happened yesterday, though the subject was approaching the centenary of his birth.

A swing from songs and piano music towards larger orchestral and choral compositions began as the Thirties opened. He entered this decade with his finest large-scale work, the *Piano Concerto*, begun in 1930 itself.

Again, any prospective biographer comes up against alternative outlines of a composition's birth. The composer's personal account, narrated when old age had mellowed him, begins with Ireland walking along a corridor at the Royal College of Music, when his career as professor for composition and piano was at its zenith. Through the half-open door of another professor's room poured a stream of spectacular piano figuration in contemporary vein. As the door hid the player from view, Ireland did not see whether a male or female pianist was in action, nor whether it was an extremely advanced student or a staff musician. All he knew was that the performer's command of this difficult music was outstanding. Listening outside Ireland thought, 'By Jove, there's a promising pianist, if it's a student.' A big 'if' remained in his mind as he walked off, while the unseen pianist continued with Prokofiev's *Third Piano Concerto.*

Next time Ireland met the professor who occupied that room he enquired, 'Is that a student of yours who plays the Prokofiev concerto?' 'Oh, yes,' replied his colleague, 'that's young Helen Perkin. She's been pestering me to get her an audition with Wood for a Promenade Concert.' His voice took on a suddenly peevish tone, as he added irritably: 'I'm NOT an impresario! I'm a professor of piano.'

Ireland's natural bent for encouraging talent set him pondering, for Helen Perkin's ability was quite out of the ordinary. 'I'll see she gets an audition for Wood,' he resolved, being in a position to negotiate it. This vow was considerably strengthened when she was sent to him for composition tuition, an essential part of a performer's training, if only to create closer understanding of the composers she would have to interpret.

The College concert at which Helen Perkin gave a brilliant public account of the Prokofiev work sparked off another idea. Ireland would not merely introduce her to Henry Wood and leave Wood to decide on a programme. His own *Piano Concerto* was already in an embryonic state, a work she could capably tackle if modifications were incorporated to suit the small span of her hands. 'I'll give her the first performance,' he spontaneously decided, despite his knowledge that many top-line soloists, including Moiseivitch, coveted this honour. As every critic in England would be present for the important premiere of his first orchestral essay since *Mai-Dun,* the attractive and youthful soloist, previously unknown, could not fail to be noticed. As the concert drew nearer and Helen Perkin's performance under the composer's own intensive coaching got into the essence of this richly romantic score, a final scheme for attracting the critics and disconcerting London's prim musical Establishment swam into his mind. It was a typical instance of quixotic Ireland devilry: 'I'll dedicate it to her, too . . . that will settle the whole business, and if she gives a good performance it will launch her on her career.'

In the tight-lipped, holier-than-thou climate of half a century ago, a 50-year-old composer who presented the dedication and premiere of his biggest work to a pretty and brilliant debutante soloist, and who lavished upon her weeks of personal coaching, must have expected to become a target of gossip, particularly the brand flourishing in such a close-knit community as a musical college. An established composer and the daughter of a staid provincial family would have raised eyebrows had they merely strolled along a corridor together, talking of nothing but crotchets and quavers. Convinced of the rightness of his campaign, Ireland chose to ignore the faceless community called 'They', of whom no more is ever known than that 'They say . . .'

He ignored the more conservative critics, too.

'I hear you are trying to get a certain effect on the trumpets in your concerto,' wrote the famous band-leader Jack Payne, whom Ireland had never met; 'If you're doing nothing on Saturday, come along and I'll get the "boys" to play all the mutes they have.' Ireland delightedly accepted. Mute after mute was tried for him until he heard the soft sound he wanted, unobtainable with the conventional brass mute. Thus a fibre-mute was specified for the first time in a score for symphony orchestra.

Ernest Newman disgustedly attacked Ireland's borrowing

from such a source. 'When a serious English composer hob-nobs with the leader of a dance-band, what hope is there for English music?' he wrote. Ireland's *Concerto,* complete with Jack Payne's mute, suggested that hope had rarely, if ever, been higher.

Following its Prom premiere Ireland's magnificent *Piano Concerto* slipped straight into the permanent piano repertoire as a welcome alternative to the over-familiar classics, with whose fervour it had a certain affinity. It would have taken the same place whoever actually first played it, so majestic, colourful and deeply felt was this music. Time's judgement places it among only a handful of masterpieces putting native music on an international footing. In the words of another leading composer: 'The *Piano Concerto* for generations to come will show to what heights English music reached in the 20th century, together with Vaughan Williams' *6th Symphony* and Elgar's *Introduction and Allegro for Strings.'*

The *Concerto's* youthful exponent, though she became for a time well known for interpretation of Ireland's music, did not stay the course for a long career. She is believed to have eloped and retired temporarily into family life. Her husband is said to have persuaded her to cut the association and cease playing Ireland's works. 'She repudiated my music' was all Ireland ever said of the affair, without enlargement. So annoyed was Ireland by this and her abandonment of an out-standingly promising career as to expunge the dedication from his score. Not for about twelve years did Helen Perkin again cross his path, by mail instead of in person, but time proved not to have healed the wound. Briefly, he mentioned to one of his wartime hostesses that a letter received that morning was from a former protegée, who had disappointed him, but who now sought his aid in making a come-back. Ireland appeared disconcerted as well as surprised when his companion innocently asked 'Is it Helen Perkin you are talking of?' he being apparently unaware of a family connection. He is described as immediately shutting up like the proverbial clam, having already asserted that he had no plan for helping her, in an uncharacteristically snappy tone. The subject was never mentioned again.

The *Concerto,* some 25 years after its completion, earned

the doubtful distinction of being performed in a concert hall thick with uniformed and plainclothes police, by a soloist under immediate threat of murder. Every Fleet Street scribe pounced on the unusual prospect of mayhem at a Prom. Presumably the basis of the threatening letter received during final rehearsals by Gina Bachauer was political rather than personal, she being of Greek extraction and the Prom coinciding with a period of Eastern Mediterranean unrest. It went straight to the point: if she appeared at the Albert Hall to play Ireland's *Concerto,* she would be shot in full view of her audience.

Although Sir Malcolm Sargent, the conductor for that evening, professed to feel reassured by so large a police presence, Madame Bachauer's English husband could visualise the audience only as 7,000 prospective assassins. He spent his time prowling the back-stage corridors. Ireland himself joined those attempting to dissuade the lady from risking her life. 'For Heaven's sake, don't play my *Concerto,*' he implored; 'I don't want you to be shot.' But the soloist courageously retorted, 'I love your music, and intend to play it.' Wails from the composer that he would never forgive himself for her death failed to move her. Doubtless they were prompted by revived memories of his own public performance of the *Sonatina* and the dirty 'I shall shoot you' threat afterwards poked through his door. In the event nothing happened, beyond a spate of excitable newspaper accounts.

Unfortunately no second piano concerto materialised, though Ireland is known to have attended a 1943 Prom specially to asssess Moiseivitch's handling of a Rachmaninoff concerto, with a work specially written for him in mind.

By the time of the *Piano Concerto* Ireland was doing well, so far as income from royalties was concerned. Nevertheless, and wisely, he retained the security of regular work as a College professor, lecturer and examiner. From his tours in the latter capacity comes an anecdote of a girl student taking an examination for which she had prepared *The Island Spell.* Her interpretation was thoroughly authentic, she took care to point out, based *exactly* upon the composer's own intentions, the examiner having questioned her in some puzzlement on certain features described as 'unusual'. He, needless to add, was John Ireland.

As a teacher Ireland's success was based to a large extent on his understanding of young people's feelings and aspirations, and on kindness and tolerance stemming from a resolve never to put them through the miseries he himself suffered as a child. 'Those ambiguous ladies called governesses' as he called them, whose duties included instilling into him an impression that music consisted of nothing but 'Beethoven, the key of "G", punishment and pain' were still fresh in his memory. He shuddered in retrospect: 'As an infant of six or seven my life was blighted – yes, positively blighted – by the simplest piece of music Beethoven ever wrote, namely his *Sonatina in G*. There were certain bits in this which my infantile fingers simply could not cope with. And every time these bits were reached, down came a sharp rap upon my knuckles with a round, black, and quite hefty ruler wielded by the worthy governess then in charge of my studies, music included. A year later I had another governess who was an even more vigorous exponent of the ruler technique. Did my difficulties vanish under this ruler treatment? No; but my terror and incompetence increased.' Ireland encountered more discipline based on fear at the Royal College itself when a tutor, suspecting skimped preparation, roared in front of a class, 'Where do you live, Mr. Ireland?' On receiving the cowed answer, 'Hampstead, Sir,' he added savagely, 'Then go home at once, practice that passage for three hours, and come straight back to me here.'

Remembering all this excellent training on how not to fire pupils' enthusiasm, Ireland aimed at awakening natural understanding. True, he drove hard when competence needed goading into the dormant virtuosity he knew was there; he drove to break indiscipline or laziness, but never to break a youngster's spirit. He encouraged individualism instead of forcing preconceived notions onto others, teaching them to be unafraid of expressing emotion through music.

None of those passing through Ireland's hands displayed more extraordinary talent than the youthful Benjamin Britten, who came before a panel including Ireland, Vaughan Williams and another adjudicator when competing for a College scholarship. Although his fellow adjudicators initially expressed doubts, Ireland bluntly affirmed, 'This is the finest musical brain that has entered this building for generations,' indicating that he favoured an award for the youth. Agreement was reached after intense discussion. After the scholarship award, Frank Bridge wrote to Ireland: 'I hear that my young protegé Benjamin Britten has won a scholarship to the RCM, and I want you to teach him.' 'I want to,' replied Ireland, 'but don't want to poach on your preserves.' Bridge was emphatic: 'I've never given the boy a lesson in his life — and if *you* don't take him I won't allow him to take up the scholarship!' Britten duly entered the College; an industrious but precociously individualistic genius, impatient to explore music to its limits almost before he had time to assimilate its traditions. Already he was reaching for the stars his elders were reluctant to stare in the face, so dazzling and strange were they. Small wonder that some had had doubts as to whether this singular character would fit into the set ways and systems of an old-established academy.

A musician of such honesty and concern for music as Ireland, though himself following very different trains of thought, never ceased to marvel at Britten's inventiveness, even if he could not actually like what he wrote. 'On Wednesday I went to both the rehearsal and performance of some music from "Peter Grimes", which Britten has made into a sort of "Suite",' wrote Ireland to a friend in 1945: 'I was very much impressed by it. He really has achieved something very remarkable here — it is quite different from anything I have heard before from him. In some respects he could twist every other composer in this country round his little finger. It was not pleasant or uplifting — rather Satanic, I thought — but very masterly indeed. Walton was there, with Lady Wimborne. He must have felt rather a draught, I fancy! (Being, so to speak, in the same line of business!!)' This implied no belittling of Ireland's friend Walton, to whom he dedicated his Third *Trio*; every composer felt a draught, whatever his own stature, when Britten's masterpiece first appeared. Ireland's view of Britten's operas did not change with the passage of time. 'I've just heard *The Taming of the Shrew*' he said in another letter; 'what Britten does with 13 instruments is brilliant. I don't *like* the music, but. . .'

The sudden production of a massive concerto after ten years' concentration on songs and piano solos inevitably set London speculating as to when Ireland would take the next conventional step and write a symphony. A major composer of fifty without one symphony to his name was unusual, but Ireland was too sincere to flash one before his public, like a conjurer materialising a rabbit from a hat, merely because it was expected of him. His response to those who raised the question was always a firm refusal: 'Everything that could be said in a symphony has already been said by Beethoven, Brahms and Elgar;' or 'You have to have a very high opinion of yourself to write a symphony;' or, to a young modern inventor of what Ireland termed plumbing-noises, 'I've never had an urge to write a symphony, and I've no urge to concoct one for the critics.'

'The first thing a student does is to write a symphony,' was his last word.

The composer never regretted resisting all blandishments to conform to convention. Listening in his final years to a broadcast series of squeaks and squawks alleged to take symphonic form, he repeated once more, 'You know, I'm glad I was never persuaded to concoct a symphony.'

Instead of 'concocting' something he felt was not in him, he turned back to Sussex for ideas. Green ways and the wild plants sheltering in their hedgerows had attracted him from boyhood, and he was still in his teens when his conception of an ideal life was set out in a letter to Mary Barlow Bentley, a music-college friend of his sister Ethel, penned during a holiday among the Lake District glories of Patterdale:

'It is very nice and quiet here. I shall be quite grieved to leave and return to that tomb in London. It is now five weeks since I left. They have gone smoothly, and the last two even pleasantly. I am writing a string quartet in C-minor. Three movements are finished and the last one is fairly started. It will be a decent work when finished, but not very exciting.

On Friday I walked to Ambleside and back by the Kirkstone Pass. I also saw a few civilized people, which rather disgusted me. I have become quite a recluse. Nothing would suit me better than to live in a comfortable cave with music paper, cigarettes and books. An electrophone [gramophone] would be all that one would need to remind one of the outer world.

On Saturday, Monday or Tuesday I shall go back to that purgatory and torture-house in London. I could use language. . .'

Presumably the tomb and torture-house referred to were the Royal College of Music, which had suddenly seemed uncongenial in comparison with his rural freedom.

Ireland was more than ever a country-lover by the second year of the 1930s, when he began translating green Sussex uplands into sound in *A Downland Suite* for brass band, an ensemble either ignored by many serious composers, or regarded by them as shallow and vulgar — appealing mainly to Bank Holiday crowds.

A Downland Suite was specially devised for one of the famous brass band contests held at the Crystal Palace, only four years before its destruction in one of London's most spectacular blazes, apart from the Great Fire of 1666 and the Blitz. Such contests were initially features of Northern life, where colliery and works bands reached — as they still do — extremely high standards. Sullivan, who conducted the massed prize bands which came down to London in 1898, was so impressed as to suggest regular Palace competition festivals. They began in 1900 with twenty bands, but, in company with cat shows, Spurgeon's evangelical rallies, Co-operative conventions and *Messiahs,* the band contests steadily grew in scale, influenced by the enormous size of the Crystal Palace itself. By the time *A Downland Suite* was written, over two hundred bands competed, comprising about six thousand enthusiastic exponents of the art of oom-pah.

Kenneth Wright, a leading brass band authority, first aroused Ireland's interest. For thus opening new creative horizons Ireland dedicated *A Downland Suite* to Wright, though its specific originator was the great band conductor Harry Mortimer, who had cleverly played upon Ireland's contradictory streak by accusing composers of artistic snobbery in a harangue ending: '*You* people don't bother about brass bands.' Ireland rose to the bait. 'All right, I'll write something for you,' he promised, 'but you'll probably never play it; you prefer to stick to your Gilbert and Sullivan.' Momentarily he had forgotten how much Sullivan had done to make brass bands respectable.

About ten years later, work began on adapting two movements from this suite — *Minuet* and *Elegy* — for conventional string orchestra. These sketches, with an unfinished manuscript of *Sarnia* and the clothes he wore, were all Ireland salvaged in his flight from an imminent Nazi invasion of the Channel Islands, in which he left behind his car, wardrobe, and all other personal possessions. Scored with time-saving help from his friend Geoffrey Bush, *Minuet* and *Elegy* were finally published in 1942. Dr. Bush has since completed the rest of this transcription.

Returning to the short piano solos he had necessarily neglected during the writing of a long concerto, Ireland produced *Indian Summer* (using thematic material which was resurrected afterwards to represent the flowering cherry tree in a suite extolling natural beauty, *Green Ways*) and *Month's Mind*. The second is a good example of the chordal writing he, rightly, detested being taken too fast. Erring on the slow side is almost always preferable with Ireland, to let his 'significant harmony' sink into the ear. The title alone is sufficient clue that *Month's Mind* should flow gently, to express grief that resigns itself into sorrowful serenity in the final bars. The published sheet-music carries a quotation from Brand's *Antiquities*: 'Days which our ancestors called their "Month's Mind", as being the days whereon their souls (after death) were had in special remembrance.' In pre-Reformation days it was the usual practice to say a Requiem Mass (or some other form of funeral Mass) exactly one month after a person's death, to remind others of their loss and of their own mortality. Writers, notably Shakespeare and Samuel Butler, adopted it to imply an overwhelming longing akin to the cravings of a woman after one month of pregnancy. Longing certainly pervades *Month's Mind*, like the urge of nature in winter to respond to earliest spring in the air.

It was such compositions that prompted Moeran to assert: 'There is ... no other living composer of pianoforte music who has contrived to say so much within the limits of a short piece of three or four pages, and to say it with such precision and fine finish of craftsmanship.'

Durham University conferred an honorary Doctorate of Music upon Ireland in 1932 — he was already a Bachelor of

Music of the same university in his own right — in recognition of his stature among contemporary composers. Even an academic honour afforded intimates of this delightfully contradictory, unconscious humourist cause for a little discreet mirth. He now forgot his previous denunciations of those who accepted honorary degrees, without working through a full degree course, as Vaughan Williams had done, and immediately insisted upon being addressed as *Doctor* Ireland.

At about the same period, the wealthy widow of a Guernsey rector decided that an appropriate memorial to her late husband would be a new organ for his church. Dr. Ireland, a friend and by long association virtually an honorary Guernseyman, was asked to draw up a specification entirely to his own liking. He accepted subject to one unusual condition for one of the great men of his day: that he should, when in Guernsey, be official organist and choirmaster of this island church.

Next on Ireland's list of works comes a short compact one-movement composition for piano, an evocation of the Sussex Downs' mystical prehistoric and historic flavour briefly titled *Legend*. It was conceived at Harrow Hill near his Ashington weekend cottage, during a lone walk in the vicinity of the Lepers' Path. This lead to a ruin known as Friday's Church from a local priest's regular Friday tramps uphill to administer the Sacrament to a leper colony, for whose benefit the chancel was equipped with a lepers' squint. Also on Harrow Hill were a small prehistoric hill-fort and a neolithic flint mine, both of them attractive to one who so revelled in ancient days.

Ireland was at first slightly irritated to discover that his chosen picnic place was not, after all, deserted. A group of children appeared before he had even unpacked his sandwiches. Suddenly, something eerie struck him: the children, though dancing happily around quite close to him, were completely silent. No voices. No laughter. No sounds of feet. Only then did he realise that they wore what he afterwards described as 'archaic clothing' of some indeterminate period long before 1933. For an instant he glanced away. When he looked again the strange children had vanished into thin air. Arthur Machen, the author whose books had so inflamed his interest in the occult and in times before recorded history began, was the obvious person to tell of this strange experience. Machen's reply to Ireland's long letter came on a postcard. It was as brief and laconic as one of Ireland's own 'Oh's,' reading simply: 'So *you've* seen them, too!'

The dancing horn theme of *Legend's* central section, taken up by the solo piano, reflects the movements of these silent children. Its mysterious opening and closing sections evoke the atmosphere of the Lepers' Path up which he had climbed before meeting them. Appropriately, *Legend* was dedicated to Machen.

A fairly rare bird as a public performer or conductor, Ireland was asked to play *Legend* himself in at least one Prom. But his boyhood aspiration to become a concert pianist was quite dead. His refusal was governed mainly by a belief that he was not a first-class performer of his own music, and by his loathing of serious practice. He could become as infuriated as a beginner when five fingers refused to cope with pages he himself had scattered with such thick note clusters as to need seven fingers on each hand. On at least one occasion he was overheard shouting 'Hell! Damn! BLAST!' to the piano.

If *Legend* and *A Downland Suite* personified the country-loving composer, *A London Overture* embodied his other, urban self; a convivial Chelsea dweller who could find music in a policeman's regulation boots or a Cockney bus conductor's rasping voice calling out 'Piccadilly!'

Both these characters appear in the overture. The bobby inhabits a mysterious foggy street, patrolling rhythmically on foot by night, whilst the busman bawls out *'Picc-a-DILL-y! Picc-a-DILL-y!'* in the opening phrase. His East End twang is far removed from the flatly refined unaccentuated 'Piccadilly' adopted in Ireland's day by some radio announcers of this piece. A glorious slow central section temporarily puts mundane matters aside in an outpouring of grief for Ireland's great friend Percy Bentham, in whose memory it was composed. Bentham's death was the more tragic for its triteness, caused by poison being absorbed into the skin from a cheap Japanese imitation of a Panama hat which he had bought during a London heatwave.

A London Overture, first played at a 1936 Prom, sprang

from another brass band sketch, rewritten with considerable elaboration.

Something of a brass band's gusto and vitality should enter the symphony orchestra if *A London Overture* is to have the cheerful Cockney flavour Ireland intended. This is clear from a letter of thanks to Barbirolli, written after a broadcast in 1956:

> 'Thank you for your *splendid* performance last Tuesday of my "London Overture". Even over wireless it was most thrilling and must have been wonderful in the hall itself. Several people have written to me about it. It was so virile and convincing — robust and really "London" in feeling. Several points were brought out which one seldom hears — I was particularly struck with the "Piccadilly" near the end on the 3 trombones and timps., which I had never heard brought out before as I intended. The opening section was impressive and the whole shape and build-up grand.
>
> I must thank you a thousand times and ask you to tell your wonderful orchestra how delighted I was, and to thank them warmly for their fine playing and the great pleasure it gave me.'

Ireland wrote no oratorio, no opera, no full length choral works; but his single shorter essay in choral writing, *These Things Shall Be,* is among his most frequently performed works. It is sometimes said to be the only one able satisfactorily to follow Beethoven's *Choral Symphony.*

These Things, as it is popularly known, sprang from a BBC invitation to produce a work for a concert celebrating the accession and coronation in 1937 of King George VI. Based on a poem of John Addington Symonds, it includes a symphonic orchestral section, heralding the magnificent statement 'These things shall be.' Up against time, with other commissions on hand, Ireland roped in his former pupil and composer friend Alan Bush to do much of the orchestral scoring, from sketches sent in sections as they were completed, with exact instructions for the instrumentation. For this service Bush was presented with the dedication.

At the BBC's coronation concert, *These Things* was straightaway recognised as an addition to the standard repertoire. Today it is still fairly regularly performed. 'It *is* beautiful music, isn't it?' Sir Adrian Boult spontaneously commented during sessions for his definitive recording.

The cantata, as a matter of interest, bears no relationship beyond its title to a hymn tune of the same name, written in 1919.

Ireland's last commission for the National Brass Band Festival at the Crystal Palace was executed in 1934; *A Comedy Overture,* largely based on the perky material he used two years later to portray London.

Only two more important creations were begun before the happy thirties were swallowed into the maw of war: a *Piano Trio* dedicated to William Walton, rewritten from a couple of early trios; and another piano suite based on nature, *Green Ways.* Each of its three movements portrays a tree: cherry, in a pensive little solo; cypress, in melody as brooding as its gloomy foliage; and, bracketed together, two English hedge-row trees of springtime, the palm or pussy-willow, and may, the countryman's name for hawthorn. Each is dedicated to a person in the composer's affections.

Number 1, *The Cherry Tree,* bears an inscription to Herbert S. Brown, a leading solicitor of Ireland's favourite Kent coast retreat. Brown, working from offices opposite the composer's weekend flat in Deal High Street, served him in two ways; as his chief legal adviser, and as a friend with whom to talk music, Brown being a highly gifted amateur whose opinions the professional composer valued. At one time a biography of Ireland from Brown's pen was discussed, tracing his life up to about the period of *Green Ways,* but it never came to fruition.

Alfred Chenhalls, dedicatee of Number 2, *Cypress,* appeared to be hurt that Ireland, much given to inscribing music to his army of friends, had not so far accorded him this honour. Having *Green Ways* in hand, Ireland forthwith redressed the omission by giving Chenhalls *Cypress.* Chenhalls, Ireland's accountant and an outstanding amateur pianist, was in two minds after playing it through beautifully at sight. Moved by its beauty and pleased at Ireland's recognition, he was nevertheless oppressed by an inexplicable foreboding so intense that he wished Ireland had not chosen this particular piece to bear his name. Perhaps it was a feeling engendered by words associating this tree with death: 'And in the sad cypress let me be laid.' Not long afterwards the film star Leslie Howard was sent to Lisbon on movie business.

John Ireland's birthplace 'Inglewood' at Bowdon, Cheshire

Annie Ireland (nee Nicholson)   Alexander Ireland

Studio portraits of the young John Ireland taken in 1880, 1882 and 1884

Two more studio portraits taken in 1886 during a visit to Blackpool

The Dame School group photograph taken in about 1887

1895

1907

1910

1920

Two holiday
snapshots
taken in Jersey
during 1910

John Ireland
loved fast
motor cars
1917

Above:
Portrait of the Composer
1917

Left:
Rock Mill 1915

Below:
John Ireland at
Rock Mill in 1954

Right:
With Eugene
Goossens in 1960

Below:
Portrait 1954

Above:
With John Hollingsworth in 1955

Photograph by Leonard Bacon c. 1943

The music room at Steyning (Photo by R. Vandyke)

Reconstruction, at Steyning, of a favourite room at Rock Mill, with original furniture. On further side of lovely polished oval table is the crack made by Ireland's fist when refusing to allow war threats to drive him to America   (Photo by Muriel V. Searle)

Above:
The upper lawn, Rock Mill commands a fine view of Chanctonbury Ring,
which inspired the Piano Concerto, Equinox and other piano pieces

Left:
Studio portrait of
the composer

Below:
A broadcast of an
interview/piano recital
with Ralph Hill, c.1943

Pen-and-ink
sketch of the
composer by
W. Powys Evans
1932

John Ireland on his 75th birthday. Radio Times photograph

With Norah Kirby at Rock Mill, and the Seal Point Siamese cat 'Smoky'

An 80th birthday portrait: August 1959. Photo by Alan Chappelow

Portrait, now at Steyning, by Arnold Mason R.A., painted in 1928

Chenhalls, a friend of this handsome actor, was invited to go with him. Lisbon was alive with spies. Unfortunately, Chenhalls bore a remarkable physical and facial resemblance to Churchill, about which friends at home often teased him. In Lisbon he was seriously taken to be Churchill himself. Word flew to German intelligence that the great Englishman in person was in Portugal and due to return on the same aircraft as Leslie Howard. 'Churchill', or rather Chenhalls, was seen to go aboard. In his classic account of the Second World War Churchill recounts the story of this plane's mid-air attack by German crews, killing both Leslie Howard and the Premier's unfortunate double. He expresses sadness for the victims, and amazement that any potential enemy should be so naive as to imagine the British Prime Minister, at such a time, would choose to travel in a civilian aircraft without escort, or to stroll so openly and unconcernedly about Lisbon airport. Ireland often thought, afterwards, upon Chenhalls' uncomfortable feeling about the *Cypress* dedication, pondering the way in which fate had linked one of his best friends with his idol, Churchill.

The Palm and May of *Green Ways* remembers Harriet Cohen, the concert pianist who was such a lovely interpreter of English music.

Cherry, cypress, palm and may all appear in the John Ireland memorial window, with marigold and other plants he pictured in music; a striking patch of greenery framing his cameo portrait, in contrast to the window's predominating blues.

Green Ways was published in 1938, the last full year of peace before Europe was plunged into the holocaust of another war. After the brief, deceptive lull of the first months of 1939, the world would change. Times would never be quite the same again, and neither would Ireland's music.

He, like the world he lived in, was about to enter a new phase.

7. The Island Spell

The story of Ireland's life now splits into three studies: such music as came out of the Second World War period; his pillar-to-post existence after leaving his beloved Channel Islands with the toe of a Nazi jackboot close behind him; and the composer as a man of humour. Records illustrating the latter trait are fuller for this time than any other, thanks to his going to earth for most of the war in the Rectory of his former St. Luke's curate. Here he found himself fitting in with evacuees, clerics, Mothers' Union ladies, children arriving for classes, and all the other visitors and callers upon a busy clerical ménage. Ireland's hostess, Mrs Marjorie Walde, wife of the Rev. Paul Walde, incumbent of Little Sampford in Essex, had the ready wit and tongue to cope with such a houseful, provided she resisted any temptation to concentrate on one person, The Great Man, to the detriment of her other charges. Fortunately she was over thirty years younger than her husband, ensuring that the memoirs of Ireland in wartime which she recounted to the author were those of an alert and light-hearted mind instead of a fellow centenarian.

War already hovered in the uncertain air of Europe when one of England's last pre-war musical gatherings went into rehearsal, the 1939 Canterbury Festival. For this Ireland's final peacetime composition, *Concertino Pastorale* for strings, was penned, a significant addition to the string repertoire. Started at his Deal retreat and completed in Guernsey, *Concertino Pastorale* was dedicated to the Festival's conductor, Boyd Neel, pioneer of string orchestras in their own right. It seemed to foreshadow the future, not specifically but in spirit; an angular opening preceded a heartbreakingly lovely *Threnody* of mourning, and a waspishly stinging final toccata.

As war became almost certain, plans were finalised for evacuating children from London and such vulnerable coastal towns as Deal. Adults with friends across the Atlantic began considering America as a haven. Ireland was implored to follow those far-sighted European musicians who were migrating there while the going was good. He, however, stood firm. 'I am *not* going to be driven out of this country by Hitler or anyone else!' he retorted, crashing his fist down for emphasis onto the edge of a solid polished table, when another well-meaning friend tried to persuade him. A long, deep crack opened straight along the grain, about an inch in. It is still visible today on this lovely oval table, maintained to a superb gloss at Steyning.

Ireland's dearly-loved Channel Islands called far more strongly than America. Neither he nor anyone else could envisage then that they would be the only British territory actually invaded and occupied by German troops. Accordingly he closed the Deal weekend flat and shut up the Chelsea studio in Gunter Grove, putting the furniture into store, before departing for an indefinite stay in Guernsey, where for a year he moved between several addresses.

Initially the worst menaces he had to face were a final wave of holidaymakers, cramming into those doomed weeks enough enjoyment to last the eternity they feared was coming, and the legions of wasps which appear to live a more intense community life in the Islands than elsewhere. Many visitors have been driven off favourite Jersey or Guernsey beaches and viewpoints by these persistent creatures. Ireland adopted the foolhardy practice of swiping out in all directions at those which, with the depraved instinct of their kind, buzzed thicker still about someone they sensed was afraid of them; and Ireland admitted he genuinely was afraid when a swarm chose to chase him. As a young organist he had given his curate friend Paul Walde great amusement as he hopped frantically and flapped wildly with a bathing towel. Grown to riper years but no more tolerant of stinging insects, his wasp dances were as hilarious as ever in 1939, as he travelled the various islands' beaches on day excursions.

From the Southampton steamer Ireland with his companion and fellow-musician John Longmire went straight to the Royal Hotel, placed almost directly on the bustling Esplanade of St. Peter Port, Guernsey's capital. For three weeks they remained there, until their rented bungalow at Jerbourg was available. Guernsey offers few lovelier spots than Jerbourg, gazing straight across Oxford-blue waters criss-crossed by passenger and cargo ships, inter-island ferries and yachts, towards Sark, Herm, and little Jethou.

Both musicians were content until the holiday rush began. Too near St. Peter Port for tranquillity, and too well-known, Jerbourg became noisy with picnicking trippers. A Boy Scout camp finished it as a place in which to think, play or compose music.

The two friends moved inland, mindful that the pleasantly undulating but unspectacular interior was more attractive to somnolent Guernsey cows than to holidaymakers. In St. Martin's parish, at a rented house unoriginally named Woodside, the musicians came to rest. Guernsey's prime attractions for Ireland were its wealth of prehistoric dolmens and barrows, and its evidence of Roman colonisation. Its Latin name was Sarnia. 'Sarnia' mused Ireland; 'a fine name for a composition'. *Sarnia,* his famous island-inspired piano sequence, was well mapped out in his mind when war was officially declared early in September, 1939.

Little warlike activity was in evidence at first. Guernsey, far from London, seemed 'comparatively safe' as he sat down on September 23rd to write to his old friend the Rev. Paul Walde:

'I came over here in July with an old pupil and his wife for a holiday, but as things are now I shall probably stay on indefinitely, as apart from "blackout" and the usual A.R.P. precautions, Guernsey is quite peaceful, and I suppose comparatively safe, although the aerodrome has been taken over by a detachment of the R.A.F. with some men and 4 or 5 warplanes which I believe are for spotting submarines, and patrol work. I am sharing this place, wh: is a small, modern, furnished house in rural or semi-rural surroundings about 1½ miles from St. Peter Port. We have taken it for at any rate 6 months. This is a very cheap way of living, whi: is a consideration, as any work I had in London has vanished, and such income as I may get from composition will be considerably decreased under war conditions − but I am rather relieved to see they are broadcasting 3

works of mine this coming week. I had 4 works down at the Promenade Concerts, and the cancellation of these concerts of course means
a serious loss to me in Performing Rights, wh: is the only source of
income a composer has.'

Despite the emergency, day-trips to the other islands were
still possible. Ireland, like humbler trippers, waxed lyrical
over Sark before returning to earth with preparations for war
in earnest:

'I have been to Sark 2 or 3 times, and that, of course, is the real gem
of the Channel Islands. There are no motorcars allowed there, so
that alone makes the place unique — and it is entrancingly beautiful
in a way of its own. . . One might feel very tempted to end one's
days there, if one could be content to be so completely cut off, as I
think perhaps I could. . . The mentality of the Islanders is shown by
the fact that the inhabitants of Sark are complaining at not having
received gas-masks — while I am sure Guernsey regards itself as the
centre of hostilities, to judge by the ridiculous fuss in A.R.P. being
made here.'

Barely six months later, Guernsey's concern with protect-
ing itself was seen as anything but ridiculous.

Even war created nostalgia in those old enough to dwell on
memories. 'This outbreak of World War II takes my mind
back to 1914, when you were taken ill, and I used to visit
you at Chigwell, do you remember?' Ireland asked his friend
of over four decades' standing. A repetition, as to other
thinking men, was a puzzle:

'The whole thing seems to me most confused and obscure . . . so
utterly diabolical that it seems like an evil dream. Is it a necessary
step in the evolution of humanity, or a case of the Gadarene swine
on a universal scale? I wonder. Luckily one does not feel at 60 as
one did when one was young and comparatively optimistic about life
generally. But it is very hard on young fellows who were looking forward to happiness and a career, such as my students, all of whom
have had to abandon their work.'

The boredom of the phoney-war crept into the slightly
pathetic postscript of a musician who had temporarily lost
his direction in life: 'I . . . shall endeavour to go on with my
work as a composer, as far as I can, and while I can. There is
nothing else to do.'

The Rector addressed in this and in subsequent wartime
letters loaned to the author is addressed as 'My dear Waldie,'

a spelling of Walde adopted on a sudden whim immediately before the clergyman's marriage, to the regret of his bride, who reverted to the normal family spelling after his death.

Balancing Maiden Castle in London's John Ireland Memorial Window is an old stone tower on a rock above spuming seas. It symbolises the half-century span of his love for the Channel Islands and the Islands' influence on so much of his music. More specifically, it shows the Martello tower near his most loved Island habitation, Fort Saumarez on the great bay of L'Eree, off Guernsey's main tourist tracks.

For six months Fort Saumarez was home to the two Johns, Ireland and Longmire; six months that produced drafts of a masterpiece in modern piano writing, *Sarnia*.

The phoney-war dragged on, neither battle nor peace, but an uneasy alternation between self-delusion and belief that the real storm had not yet broken. Neither natives nor long-term mainlander residents like Ireland and Longmire fully appreciated the archipelago's vulnerability, should neighbouring France fall, as a springboard to parts of England less heavily fortified than the cliffs of Dover. Ireland, with 'nothing else to do', began reshaping the two *Downland Suite* brass band extracts for strings, and putting *Sarnia: An Island Sequence* onto paper.

When they were finally completed at Banbury in Oxfordshire, where Ireland retreated after fleeing Guernsey in the confusion of impending invasion, each of *Sarnia's* three movements bore a dedication to an Islander friend. *Le Catioroc*, portraying the hauntingly desolate area whose focal point was a dolmen-crowned outcrop to which Ireland often drove out to watch sunset over the off-islands, was inscribed to Alfred Sebire. He was a prominent Guernsey flautist who took part in a wartime Red Cross concert devoted to Ireland's music and, after peace returned, was among those invited to the composer's final home in Sussex.

Song of the Springtides, exuberantly dashing like seas smacking against the rocks which have made Guernsey a notorious graveyard for ships, was dedicated to Mrs. Mignot, the clergy widow at whose invitation the composer had the joy of designing a new Guernsey church organ to his own specification. Given such a golden opportunity it was a foregone conclusion that he would reproduce the magnificent registration of Holy Trinity, Sloane Street, in London, the scene of his very youthful sub-organist debut into professional music and his *beau ideal* of the perfect organ.

Between these movements of *Sarnia* comes *In A May Morning*, 'to be played as if it was so beautiful you could hardly bear it'. The single name Michael appears at the top of page one, representing Michael Rayson, small son of the owner of Birnam Court Hotel in Guernsey to which Ireland migrated when the tenancy of Fort Saumarez ended in April, whilst Longmire temporarily returned to the mainland. In his large airy room at the hotel he continued with *Sarnia* and also a new setting of the Canticles, known to choirmasters simply as *Ireland in C,* and plied his friends at home with long letters tightly packed with the small script once called, like his explosive youthful self, tigerish. Typical of these is one penned from Birnam Court to Paul Walde. It is worth quoting at length, as it deals with three different topics: the niceties of church music composition, expounded to the clergyman, who had asked Ireland's advice; the thoughts of a composer who has always been at heart a church organist; and the approach of Guernsey's invasion under the Swastika flag.

Walde had been trying his hand at what he, erroneously, thought the easiest way for a churchman to tackle composition, with three Anglican chants. Boldly he had despatched them to the famous composer asking his candid opinion. Ireland's reply ran:

'Fancy you blossoming out into composition at this period of your life! Well, Verdi did his best work at the age of 80, so you may yet become a famous composer!! I am enclosing . . . comments on the music, which I hope you will not regard as offensive or snubbing on account of their frankness. The chants interest me very much, as something proceeding from a cultured and imaginative mind in a medium very *inexpertly* handled — as if, for instance, I were to endeavour to try to express myself in paint (which I wish, above all, I could). To write a *good* double chant is extremely difficult — even the efforts in this line of the great Elgar are quite ineffective and unsatisfactory. The best essays in this direction seem to have been done, not by great or noteworthy composers, but by cathedral organists of the 18th and early 19th centuries. I should advise you, as a hobby, to make a study of harmony, including the actual structure of chords, their proper sequence, and correct and smooth part-writing. A good double chant, once more, is difficult to write, because it is a sort of *multum in parvo* — like a good aphorism. There is so little space in which to function. Also, I am convinced that you do not actually *hear* the harmonic effect of some of the chords and progressions you use. Music is primarily *sound*; written notes are only symbols, or directions for performance, and you have to hear the effect clearly with the inner ear — you cannot work it out mathematically, like a problem in algebra or geometry, tho' it may bear some relation to these things. But at any rate it is easy to see you are aiming at "something" in these chants — they are not just chaotic tosh like most music by the amateur composer. Seeing these (the chants) makes me almost inclined to buy a box of paints and see what I could do, just for fun — rotten though it would be!'

Ireland at this time was very much attuned to church music, hence his great patience in analysing a friend's untrained attempt to write music instead of sticking to what he was professionally trained to do — preach sermons, baptise infants, and sing Evensong. He was frankly enjoying himself as organist of a ritualistic Guernsey church. No author can better his own semi-humorous account of life at St. Stephen's:

'You may be amused to hear that I have been induced, by supplications, threats and cajolery, to become, more or less informally, Director of Music at the only ritualistic church on the island. For a long time I have felt I wd. like to play the organ again and to handle a choir, not too strenuously — and I was influenced by the fact that at this church (S. Stephen's) there is a splendid up-to-date 3-manual Walker organ, with all-electric action, which no local organist has ever been able to tackle, except with disastrous results — also, as you know, Popery has always had a strong appeal for me, and in the morning services we are thoroughly Popish, with the Mass in most of its glory. The music is simple, being mostly plainsong (the only *real* church music), the choir is rather weak, but inoffensive, the work is light, I have a capable assistant (a London musician who is here), and an excessively wealthy woman has put up the salary which, though not large as London goes, helps to pay my hotel bill. I enclose the local rag's announcement of this fact! . . . I have 12 boys, 4 women contraltos (these very good) about 10 women sopranos (moderate) and only 3 men, who, alas, leave a good deal to be desired. Most of the organ (great, swell and pedal) is in the west gallery, and the choir sit in a space in the middle of it — the choir organ and console are in the chancel. We have vestments, lights, incense (lots of this), reservation [of the Sacrament] and the Mass performed in a highly efficient manner from the stage-managing point of view. The servers and acolytes are drilled to every movement and every inch. It is a change from the hypocricy and banality of St. Luke's Chelsea — also from the frantic "Heath Robinsonish" organ I had there to play on (Which, by the way, was replaced, soon after I left in 1926, by a large Compton organ of the standard cinema type!)'

Ireland was not to know that invasion was scarcely a week away, as he went on to ponder the whys and wherefores of war in general:

'. . . we are well in the soup, thanks to Baldwin, Macdonald, . . . Chamberlain and the rest, and our native laziness and rooted objection to facing unpleasant facts. . . Other empires have fallen, so why not ours? . . . and even if an enemy victory means Satan let loose on earth for 1,000 years, is not this prophesied in the Scriptures? I am no defeatist, and firmly believe that in the end the Allied cause will triumph — but meanwhile things are going to be very bad. If the Germans get as far as Cherbourg (at wh: they are aiming) these islands will be of great strategic importance, and I have no illusions, current here, that we shall not be attacked, and even annexed, in the C.I., and maybe quite soon.'

Life, despite Ireland's increasing unease, had its compensations. Good friends were all around, not least a lady for whom he had long nursed a soft spot. 'Do you know any people called Hutcheson, in your neighbourhood?' he asked Walde; 'One of the sisters, Gweneth, was once quite a flame of mine; and of 2 other well-known composers also!!' The old flame was none other than she who inspired him to insert the notes C, A, D — cad! — into his piano *Sonatina* when Bax, one of the 'other composers', diverted her attentions to himself.

When John Longmire returned from England in May, another mutual friend and ex-pupil came with him, Percy Turnbull. The trio looked forward to days of conviviality, composition and island-hopping, with church appointments and examining to buy their wartime-quality daily bread. Turnbull fondly imagined he was sailing towards several weeks' well-deserved rest. He and Longmire took local rooms, whilst Ireland stayed on at Birnam Court.

June had one week to run when the three friends were put to dramatic flight. Nazi invasion was imminent. The fate of all non-native males found on the islands would be deportation to German concentration camps. Ireland, Longmire and Turnbull could take only a handful of belongings, leaving behind all other possessions, including Ireland's car. Ireland, instinctively, grabbed his unfinished manuscripts of the two *Downland Suite* transcriptions and *Sarnia* before making for the rickety, overcrowded ferry *Antwerp,* one of the last ships to escape. This tiny ferry, built for five hundred, carried three times as many jammed in with little food or water, and dogged most of the way by prowling submarines. Two babies were born aboard, and many passengers became seasick. Lurching at anchor off Weymouth in rough seas was worse than the crossing itself. Ireland needed little prompting to turn the miseries of *mal-de-mer* into such alarming symptoms that the captain was thankful to despatch him, with his companions, ashore in a tender with the women and children. The Dorset of Hardy and *Mai-Dun* had never looked sweeter to any of them.

The Island Spell that had held Ireland to itself was interrupted but not broken. In his heart he knew that, some day, the war would end. He would then lose no time in returning.

Meanwhile, however, he was virtually homeless. Gunter Grove in Chelsea was closed down and the furniture stored, under constant bombing threat. Deal was in the thick of Hell Fire Corner. As a start he migrated to Radlett, to stay with his composer friend Alan Bush, whose mother, always referred to by Ireland as Old Mrs. Bush, soon took him over. She was a woman of strong character, whose notion of nourishment was eternal baked beans: 'Very *good* for you, Dr. Ireland, very *good* for you.' Of her he went in unashamed awe. Escaping Old Mrs. Bush and her ready tin-opener, Ireland retreated to a parish near Banbury, expecting to stay with yet another clergyman friend and his sister. But the sister having recently died, the priest had left his parsonage for a small house in a 'mean' Banbury street, where he was ministered to by a dragon housekeeper and supervised by her unpleasant-natured dog.

All the unfortunate Mr. Compton, another former St. Luke's curate, could offer was a basement bedroom. It lacked even a piano for the first five months. Nevertheless, Ireland was able to complete *Sarnia* at Banbury, and work on a further piano trilogy, *Three Pastels*.

In one of their last mail exchanges to and from Guernsey, the Rev. Paul Walde had asked Ireland's advice on his own amateur psalm chants. Now the process reversed, with Ireland drawing upon the clergyman's scholarly expertise with one of his *Pastels* in mind:

> 'Forgive me for bothering you, but as you are the only classical scholar I know, I must ask you for some information. Is it correct to refer to HYACINTHUS as the mythical person referred to in the following lines:—
>
> A Grecian lad, as I hear tell,
> One that many loved in vain,
> Looked into a forest well
> And never looked away again.
> There, where the turf in springtime flowers,
> With downward eyes and gazes sad,
> Stands amid the glancing showers
> A jonquil, not a Grecian lad. (A E Housman)
>
> Or should it be *Narcissus*? The reason I want to know is, that I have quoted the first quatrain of the above as a "caption" to a piano piece, which I have named "Hyacinthus", and I don't want to become a target for the critics!'

Always a stickler for poetic exactitude, thanks to his refined literary upbringing, Ireland finally decided to compromise, according to a sequel penned from Banbury at the ungodly hour of 5.30 a.m.:

> 'My dear Walde,
> Many thanks for your informative letter dated August 25th. Acting on your exposition of the "Boy and Pool" matter, I have cut out all the names of the mythical lads, and simply called my piece "A Grecian Lad" — quoting the Housman lines — which should make clear to any but the densest that the beautiful Narcissus is the inspirer of the music.'

Peacetime Channel Island days already seemed so unreal that, in the same letter, Ireland appealed for loan of some Jersey snapshots, hoping they might restore lost trains of creative thought: 'I really am anxious to recapture some of the essence of those days — it would help my work, the basis of which is becoming more and more retrospective in its inspiration. This must needs be so, as the present state of things fills me with nothing but loathing and horror.'

Happier days were to come, foreshadowed in a tentative acceptance of Walde's invitation to stay awhile with him and his younger wife at Little Sampford rectory in Essex. Ireland wrote:

'Now, in regard to your suggestion that I should pay you a short visit — this is very kind, and in many ways I should be delighted — but I have a very queer Freudian complex about staying in other people's houses: do you mind telling me if there would be anyone except you and your wife living in the house: and . . . could I work *uninterruptedly* for some hours a day — I should need a room with a piano, a table, and a chair in it — (I am doing a longish orchestral March for the B.B.C., against time, and *must* get the blasted orchestration finished) — and could I get up and make myself a cup of tea at 6 a.m., as I can never, by any chance, sleep after 5 or 5.30 a.m. — and lastly, what about Hitler's planes? and his *bombs*? do you get many of these round about? And what about the food difficulty which my presence would create? I can bring a ration book, of course — but that means nothing, in these days. I am a small eater, however. . .'

By September 1941, though greatly appreciating Compton's kindness in offering a share of his humble Banbury dwelling, Ireland was becoming restive. He had had more than enough of a housekeeper reminding him of the train of black-clad griffins who, from babyhood onwards, had helped create his reserve towards most woman. 'I have suffered *365 days less 9,* in this rather difficult environment,' he wrote to Walde; 'The household here is ruled by a good lady housekeeper who, in the old days, you would most certainly have called a *FEEEMALE* [this word in half-inch capitals, underlined] — the bed I have to sleep on here could hold 4 people (which, in my case, is unnecessary); moreover it resembles, in many respects, a heap of rubble, to my old bones. . .'

The reference to 'a longish orchestral march' written at Banbury was not a case of a correspondent forgetting the title of his own music. The score *had* no name. By April 1942 it was complete but still nameless. *Heroic March* was jettisoned, too like Beethoven's *Eroica*; Ireland almost settled for an uninspired *March in C-minor* before adopting the title *Epic March* without enthusiasm. As *Epic March* it was premiered by Sir Henry Wood. The beauty of its central theme created a greater impression than the predictable excitement of the flanking sections. It was still going strong at the war's end in 1945. 'Yes, there really was a stupendous reception at the Albert Hall on the 25th thanks, probably, to the Atom Bomb!' he enthused a few days before Japan capitulated. 'They are broadcasting "Epic March" next Saturday, I think — but that will not be so thrilling.' With peace the march, its patriotic purpose gone, fell into neglect.

From Banbury friendships were made or renewed with Thomas Dunhill, writer of many attractive songs and teaching pieces; Walter Trinder, organist of Christ Church, South Banbury; and Geoffrey Furnish, another organist. Like schoolboys 'doing each others' dags', they derived immense pleasure from such harmless evening pursuits as each producing a setting of *Ride a cock horse to Banbury Cross*.

Ireland and Trinder formed a foursome with Balfour Gardiner and Thomas (later Sir Thomas) Armstrong. Regularly this quartet met to dine and wine at the Mitre in Oxford before adjourning to more sober occupations, such as attending choral Evensong at Christ Church cathedral. One service is still vivid in Sir Thomas' memory. As he recounted it to the author:

> 'I recall particularly an Evensong at Christ Church when we arranged for all the music to be Ireland's. We sang his C-major service, the anthem "Greater Love", and I played organ music by him and extemporized for quite a long time on themes from his music. Balfour had a too-kind opinion about my extemporization, and stood beside me urging me on to fresh effort. Ireland was very much moved, and wrote me a lovely letter about it, but alas! I've lost it.'

Writing immediately to any musician whose performance had moved or impressed him was a common practice with Ireland, almost to the last. Many famous musicians still treasure examples of these letters.

One day in 1940 the Rev. Paul Walde said casually to his wife, Marjorie, 'I think I'll go and look up old John in Banbury.' The outcome was the invitation to their Rectory at Little Sampford, near the celebrated beauty-spot of Finchingfield, which Ireland took up in the following autumn. He got no further than the doorstep of the mellow Georgian house before its atmosphere struck him. '*This* is a gracious house,' he exclaimed; 'I could *work* here.' He came again at Christmas in 1941. In his letters he thereafter continued hinting and wheedling on the 'I could work here' theme.

In April 1942 Ireland moved into Little Sampford Rectory for good. For the Waldes the next three years were to be the most interesting and laughter-filled of their lives, spent in close contact with this contradictory and often comical genius.

Because Marjorie Walde had only average musical training and executant ability, though her appreciation of music was keen, she saw Ireland as a man rather than a celebrity. To her sure memory, observation, and Irelandian sense of the ridiculous the author owes an insight into the non-musical side of his character.

From the start he was just John, in accordance with a note written before sunrise in September, 1941, from Banbury: 'This letter is addressed to you both — Paul and Marjorie — and, to you both, please, I am always *John* — not *Doctor* or *Mister* Ireland.' Thereafter he usually signed himself plain John, or with the colophon familiar to all his friends — the distinctively sloped initials J.I.

Previous visits, which were in effect reconnaisances, had proved they could all live amicably together. 'It has been a real joy to be your guest at Little Sampford,' he wrote when accepting their invitation for Christmas 1941. Directly the idea of permanent residence was mooted he proposed a businesslike footing: 'I should like to come for a longer period, if you can bear it,' he wrote soon after Christmas, 'but in that case you really must let me come as a "p.g." [paying guest]. I will undertake not to get in anybody's way, and I shall have plenty to do, so will not need any entertaining.'

For the over-worked first lady of the house and parish, he was just an extra body squeezed in under abnormal conditions. With a large rambling house on her hands, she could not neglect her normal duties to look after him. There was no resident staff, only one staunch daily help and a part-time gardener. To all the traditional duties carried out by the wife of a vicar or rector were now added the care of refugees from bombing raids, war savings groups to organise, the running of the local branch of the Mothers' Union and the comings and goings of her own pupils three or four mornings a week.

'I couldn't lionise him, even if I'd been that way inclined, and I am not, but I did value the experience and all it taught and gave me,' Mrs. Marjorie Walde told the writer. One suspects that Ireland, slightly uneasy when at the mercy of any woman with nobody else to distract her attention, liked Mrs. Walde for this very reason. She was fond of him as a person but not overawed by his fame; a clergy-wife and therefore, in old-fashioned parlance, safe.

Lacking the self-esteem of some leading musicians, Ireland fitted well into this sometimes frenetic environment. Marjorie Walde, for her part, came to admire this modesty in her additional guest quite as much as his music. He was, 'without personal pride or pomposity, disliking being lionised, though naturally desiring musical recognition and sometimes feeling it was denied him . . . never two-faced; sincere; kindly . . . never dandified or conceited . . . not a bit of a socialite.'

Best of all, Ireland brought to that war-strained household something desperately needed by all in 1942: a permanent fount of comedy to relax overwrought minds and anxious spirits. His play-acting and uninhibited tomfoolery when in expansive mood were even more amusing than 'John's funny little ways'.

Described as 'a marvellous mimic', his exact reproduction complete with slight Cockney twang of 'Old Timber' (more reverently, Sir Henry Wood) conducting a Prom rehearsal, never failed to dispel the gloom of a bad news broadcast. Mrs. Walde soon developed a useful anti-Hitler tactic: a request for 'Old Timber' when Big Ben's chimes heralded extra despair.

One source of homely humour was Ireland's gentle haggling over the rent, probably an instinctive throwback to the boyhood phase of being made accountable to a guardian for every penny spent. This had left traces of monetary exactitude which an outsider might have taken for meanness. Mrs. Walde preferred to shrug it off with 'It was fun — it was *John!*' when recounting how he carefully deducted the cost of two tupenny-ha'penny stamps, bought at her request, from his fortnightly four guineas. At the start he caused much private amusement to his hostess by trying to beat down her stated two guineas (£2.10) weekly for a pleasant wing of the Rectory, fuelling of fires and coke stoves, and all food, to a flat £2. Gamely she stood out for two guineas, payable fortnightly, with nothing refunded if he was away a few days, for which she compensated by entertaining his many musical visitors as though they were her own personal friends. It was a good bargain. Ireland capitulated, but continued religiously to deduct the cost of small purchases from the village, exactly as his guardians had once done to himself. The merry climax (without laughter to his face), came one Christmas when Ireland found gifts from the Waldes on the table, whilst he had none for them. 'You need not pay me for those cigarettes I bought you last week,' he magnanimously announced. 'My sense of humour thought this funny, rather than mean. It was just John!' repeated Mrs. Walde.

'It was just John.' This phrase, affectionately spoken, cropped up regularly during conversations and correspondence concerning this book. It was 'just John' to write, before accepting an invitation to share such a welcoming home, setting out his requirements and expectations: 'It would be as well to get in some coal, and oil, for as you know, I am a rather chilly person. I expect I should want the table in that room to work at . . . and please be sure to get the piano put in tune, wh: of course I will pay for.'

The composer kept his promise not to disturb others at those un-Christian hours when his wakefulness demanded activity and/or a cup of tea, which he brewed for himself, still clad in a dressing gown. His hosts had had ample warning in the way he dated one letter '6 a.m., September 26th' and continued: 'I could not sleep after 5, and no early tea is available, so I am spending the time by writing to you and Paul.' His matutinal teamaking forays were to leave many a laugh in the Waldes' hearts.

Parishioners and villagers were naturally curious about the Rector's guest. Children who arrived for coaching by the Rector's wife, an established teacher, were eager to glimpse him or be able to boast of meeting and speaking to the famous Dr. John Ireland. He neither liked these small girls, another of the Rectory's distractions as part of the War Effort, nor to be seen by them.

As he normally breakfasted in a dressing gown, the comedy of a famous composer in *déshabillé* hastily retreating up the back stairs to avoid meeting the children in the front hall enlivened many weekday mornings. 'Another cause for laughter' recalled Mrs. Walde, 'I can see him now, scuttling up those back stairs, at the huge Rectory, to escape from them.' She added a thought any cleric could have taken for a sermon: 'To live on like this, in the minds and memories of others, is certainly NOT to die.'

Then there was the droll drama of the 'faithful but formidable' daily help, Mrs. Balls, known affectionately to the Rector as Ma Balls except, of course, to her face.

Ma Balls revered every pink-hued brick, proudly scrubbing endless hard corridors and floors. Clad in voluminous pinafores, a ramshackle beret and heavy black boots, she led church-cleaning parties like Boadicea at the head of the Iceni. 'That old man upstairs' was of no interest to her. She had no idea that he was famous and would have been unimpressed if she had been told. Ireland had even less regard for Ma Balls, pointedly working in his room rather than downstairs whenever she was in the house. A man of such perception could hardly have failed to sense her disapproval of himself even without realising her main reason. Ma Balls, having long ago signed the Pledge, had noted the visitor's slightly bemused mien on some occasions when leaving Wiffin's Coach, a local link with Saffron Walden in the days when Ireland's evacuated BBC friends haunted its many hostelries. Finally, the good lady brought her complaint into the open, after cleaning out 'that old man's bedroom'. 'He's got some *bottles* up there,' she moaned. Marijuana sprouting on the windowsill, or a corpse under the bed, could scarcely have offended more her Band-of-Hope sensibilities.

Every Tuesday Ireland took the coach for Saffron Walden to talk shop at the Rose and Crown (tragically burned down one Boxing Night after the war, with the loss of several lives). BBC people had been evacuated to nearby Arkesden: Julian Herbage, one of his closest companions, was among them.

Meanwhile at home, Marjorie Walde had more mundane things to organise, such as feeding a hungry household on rations plus such produce as countrymen in the congregation could provide as gifts. At the time of Ireland's arrival she was a good plain cook, capable of producing pastries for church socials and of roasting Sunday lunches. He left her a better chef than she dreamed possible.

Cooking was his favourite relaxation. 'It was a form of composition — a form of creativity — he was as meticulous about what he put into his inside as about what he put into his music,' said Mrs. Walde.

Every day Ireland would ask what was for lunch and dinner, and would follow her into the kitchen to taste unfinished dishes and to enjoy 'concocting' them as painstakingly as if they were symphonies. 'I learned to cook pretty much to his liking and under his supervision,' his hostess congratulated herself.

Sauces, salads and soups intrigued him. 'His soufflés and omelettes were as fine as any French chef could achieve' confirmed one who knew Ireland as chef a little later in life; 'It was the delight of luncheon guests to watch him (through the dining room/kitchen hatch) dressing the salad, measuring each ingredient with meticulous care, and the mixing thereof before bringing it to the table.' Curiously, a volume on his elder brother Alleyne was recently discovered in a second-hand shop. Alleyne Ireland's capacity for producing exceptionally delicious salad dressings is mentioned. Coincidence, or a brotherly skill inherited from some unknown forefather? Certainly neither taught the other, for John Ireland was but an infant when Alleyne ran away to sea at sixteen, before settling for life in America, where he built up a reputation in authorship and journalism, following his father's literary footsteps. The brothers never met again.

Soup appeared nightly on the Little Sampford Rectory table, war or no war. Ireland insisted on it. He pottered into the kitchen at preparation times adding flavourings and giving out tips. Only once was this ritual disturbed when, returning late from an afternoon Mothers' Union meeting, Mrs. Walde decided to dispense with this course.

Ireland walked into the dining room, stared silently at the table from the doorway, and remarked flatly: 'H'm. No soup spoons. No soup,' and went out. Reasonably she explained that an overworked wife responsible for parish affairs as well as a large home occasionally had no time for soup-making after a long Mothers' Union session. 'It seems to me that you think more of those mothers than you do of *Me!*' he retorted, capitalising the Me in his tone of voice. His hostess, kind-hearted but, on her own admission, sharp-tongued, was not browbeaten. The Lord she answered, doubtless considered these ladies of equal importance to a famous composer, if it be true that all are equal in the sight of God. This was not their last domestic skirmish; but, despite the lady usually achieving woman's traditional last word, they 'never left any rancour on either side'.

Looking back, in physical decline, Ireland finally apologised to her: 'I'm sure . . . that I was rather a pig at Sampford, worrying you over food matters. It was most wicked of me, and now I am punished by being able to eat very little!'

He need not have worried. 'No soup spoons, no soup' is graven with a chuckle on the mind of one who treasures the unique experience of having a composer in the kitchen.

Chatting with Marjorie Walde about those years, hilarious became an over-used word. It was the only one truly apposite to such tales as the episode of the ducks.

Having farmers in their congregation, the Rectory family did better than townsfolk in supplementing their ration book allowances. Here a cabbage, there some eggs, or a pound of plums, found their way to the table. One Sunday it was a fine plump chicken, dismembered with satisfaction at lunchtime. The Rector and his wife felt more than replete. Their guest left the table to amble across to a window looking onto a charming Essex scene featuring grass, trees, and a pond on which swam a handful of rather unalluring ducks, paddling with the disinterested air of birds past their prime. 'Isn't it about time we had one of those ducks?' he enquired. His hurt expression, as people more familiar than he with ducks burst out laughing, only intensified their amusement. 'Those ducks are about a hundred years old,' gasped Mrs. Walde. In less exaggerated terms, they were elderly enough to have tasted like a cleric's cassock if roasted. Years later, when he was living in Sussex, poultry inspired a typical Ireland juxtaposition of the sublime (music) and the ridiculous (cackling hens). Having discovered that the flavourless flesh of post-war chickens and the colourless yolks of their eggs stemmed from the 'revolting cruelty' of battery farming, which he as an animal lover deeply abhorred, he was delighted to find that a favourite butcher in Steyning still supplied free-range birds and eggs, together with Norfolk ducks as a true cook liked to receive them, complete with heads and feet. Whilst enjoying one of these in company with Harold Rutland, a fellow musician, the ageing Ireland looked up with his old mischievous grin and remarked in dry, mock-professorial tones: 'It is far more meritorious to roast a bird like this than to concoct a symphony.' The word concoct, for him, was as firmly attached to the word symphony as the beak to the said bird.

Absence from Little Sampford made the heart fonder of country vegetables, as Ireland realised when business unavoidably took him to London. Writing from the Savage Club, his Gunter Grove home being still unusable, he added a P.S.: 'Tell the "Bish" [bishop] that the vegetables here are beneath contempt both for quality and quantity.'

Then there was the strawberry jam incident. A new pot of strawberry jam given to the Waldes by a parishioner was a real treat in wartime. Reposing on the tea-table, it brought back memories of plenty. Suddenly Ireland recalled that the friend with whom he had escaped from Guernsey was due for a visit. 'Mind you put that strawberry jam away before John Longmire comes,' he instructed, 'or he'll think *he* can have some of it.'

Inside most grown men is a small boy; and when that small boy pops to the surface of a genius he is doubly amusing. A good instance, told to the author with immense mirth that had nothing of malice in it, is a tale which, if it were a short story, should be entitled *The Butter Incident*. Ireland, as a ritual, always took afternoon tea following a regular nap. On Sundays there was sometimes a half-pound of pure butter, slipped surreptitiously into the Rector's car by a churchwarden. Mrs. Walde fairly divided it exactly into three, allocating one portion to Ireland to eat all at once or to conserve as he chose. Like Oliver Twist, once his third was gone he always asked for more. One Sunday his hostess relented and put extra at his place, but he suddenly turned petulant, saying 'I won't have it — you didn't *want* me to have it.' The Rector calmed him down, but not before she had overheard a voice inside the study reiterating, 'But She said. . .' Once more a youthful expression surfaced; the blanket-term 'She' for any woman of strong enough character to govern him. Temporarily a woman showing him nothing but kindness, and too safely married to a parson to have designs on his freedom, became She.

Fleeting altercations apart, Ireland greatly appreciated the Rev. and Mrs. Walde's generosity in welcoming all the musical visitors turning up at their door: critics, writers, performers and fellow composers. John Longmire, of the strawberry jam incident, came when vacations allowed escape from his school music duties at Bromsgrove. Ralph Hill and Peter Creswell (producer of *Julius Caesar*) came, as did Ireland's many friends broadcasting from Banbury, Bedford, Evesham and other locations described over the security-conscious air as 'somewhere in England'.

At over sixty, his Chelsea-bred conviviality was dulled neither by time nor by Rectory life. Little Sampford's favourite anecdote from the Rose and Crown deserves another headline, *The Slectric Iron Incident*, over Marjorie Walde's subtitle, *Another John Chuckle*.

It being impossible to improve upon her own eye-witness account, we reproduce it here, verbatim:

'He returned from one of those jolly lunches at the Rose and Crown, Saffron Walden, with his Arkesden BBC cronies, coming somewhat unsteadily into the kitchen where I was coping with the ironing (*no* electricity, so the flat irons, old style, were heated on the huge kitchen coal range); and he said: "Hullo, Marjorie. Is that your new 'slectric iron'?" Speech somewhat slurred after this jolly time. My sister who was there too, and I, were convulsed with laughter after he had gone out of the kitchen (John had retired to his afternoon rest — a ritual).

'Now I *have* an electric iron, I nevertheless always call it, to myself, my "*slectric* iron".'

Wiffin's coach, boarded at the door, was Ireland's usual transport to and from Saffron Walden. In its jolting interior he and the suspicious, rigorously teetotal Ma Balls were often fellow passengers. A London trip involved the long-distance

Jennings' Coaches (also chartered for Mothers' Union outings), plus a lift to the bus stop in the Rectory car. Only musical business lured him to that bomb-blasted city, most usually broadcasting affairs; but occasionally a personal appearance brought him to town. Outstanding among the latter was a concert in the Royal Exchange — similar to those given by Myra Hess at the National Gallery — with that master of the viola, Lionel Tertis.

If Ireland was involved in anything chuckles always seemed to come out of it. Mrs. Walde's account delightfully recreated the weeks of planning when Ireland (becoming very slightly deaf, and therefore disliking the telephone) and Tertis (rather deafer) inveigled her into acting as go-between for them, repeating what Tertis said to Ireland, standing beside her, and shouting his answer back to Tertis. Neither party could agree at first to waive his fees, as requested, this being a charity concert. It was done not for parsimonious reasons, but because Ireland in particular felt that creating such a lead might encourage promoters to expect others to play for nothing, causing hardship to young emergent performers battling against wartime odds and genuinely needing money.

Ireland's rooted objection to practising loomed larger than bombs in letters mentioning his London business trips. 'It is a nuisance that I have an engagement to play for the BBC . . . wh: will mean having to practice, and rehearse in London' he grumbled just before moving into Little Sampford. For the next four years it was repeated with the monotony of a rondo theme chasing itself through a sonata. Chairing a BBC panel monthly was more congenial, in that spot-on technique was less important. When London bombing was at its height the BBC thoughtfully travelled to him in Essex, saving him the risky overnight journey; a measure of the Corporation's valuation which contradicted his own belief that it neglected him.

As younger composers drew away from the melodic and harmonic values on which his generation had always built, he became still more sensitive to every real or imagined suggestion of neglect. 'Look, what do you think of this?' he often asked Mrs. Walde, pottering into the Rectory kitchen and thrusting under her floury hands one of many 'savage letters to the BBC', stabbed out on his hapless typewriter. Diplomatically she would suggest toning down its venom. Like an obedient boy he usually tore up the letter and started again. A stream of longer, more personal missives kept the village post office in regular business.

Ireland never was a facile composer. 'Composition is a terribly slow process' he reminded the Rev. Paul Walde before finally coming to live with him. *Epic March,* he wrote, 'cost . . . an immense amount of labour.' At Little Sampford he always seemed busy, completing this, altering that, or broadcasting as pianist from the BBC's wartime retreat of Evesham, mainly to Latin America. Friends of his 'tigerish' youth described him as pounding the piano and singing aloud as he worked; but at the Rectory, with all manner of folk going in and out, he felt it more diplomatic to guard his thoughts. Scarcely a sound came from his room when he was composing, not even from the piano.

Current commissions included incidental music for the BBC production of *Julius Caesar,* 'concocted' rather than composed, his subtle way of differentiating between inspired music and commissioned orders. Producing nearly twenty numbers in a stipulated time proved hard work. Just before the Guernsey invasion, incidentally, Ireland had spoken of this play with much admiration, appending one of musical history's most maddening remarks: 'Now there's a subject for an opera!' No opera ever materialised.

Other wartime works, wholly or partially produced in Essex, included *A Maritime Overture,* his sole essay for military band (not to be confused with a brass band), based on unpublished early sketches; a *Miniature Suite* for organ, likewise using very youthful material, reworked; and the important *Fantasy Sonata for Clarinet and Piano* expressly composed for Frederick Thurston, soloist and mainstay of London's best orchestral wind-sections, for whom was also written the central slow section of the *Satyricon* overture, surely one of the most lovely episodes for a solo woodwind instrument penned by an Englishman.

In 1944 occurred Ireland's 65th birthday, bringing him to an age when famous musicians can reckon to be commemorated publicly for their achievements, and thereafter at five-yearly intervals. A year or so before this Vaughan Williams' 70th anniversary was marked by the BBC, to a rather greater extent. In private another of those entertaining contretemps described at Little Sampford as 'just John' was the result. Pointing out that 'they'll do the same for *you* when you're seventy' failed to pacify him, despite the fact that the long-running *Music Magazine,* broadcast on Sundays, was to carry a worthy amount of Ireland air-time. 'I won't *listen*!' he snapped. As the Sunday drew nearer, however, curiosity got the better of him. 'Marjorie; will you be listening to *Music Magazine*?' he asked with exaggerated casualness. She would not: Sunday for a vicar's wife was Sunday. Ireland dithered awhile before coming out with another idea: 'Do you think your sister might be likely to listen to *Music Magazine*?' She might, but keeping him on tenterhooks was irresistible. At five minutes to eleven, the programme's starting time, Ireland shut himself into his radio-less room, ostentatiously keeping his vow not to listen. But directly the programme ended he was down again, boyishly impatient to know what had been said about him.

Memories like this made wartime joyful instead of harrowing for the Walde household. They had as much to lose as to gain when the war in Europe ended, meaning that eventually Ireland would return to London.

Ireland began renewing old friendships with people and places but he still returned regularly to Essex, until his Gunter Grove house could be repaired. The first old favourite he revisited was Deal, only a month after Germany's surrender. Battered, bombed and barbed-wired, the town still exerted its familiar pull. 'It is a strange experience to see Deal again after so long — and the *sea*' he wrote home (i.e. to Little Sampford).

Sadly, however, it was becoming apparent that his host of the past four years, Paul Walde, was far from well. It was time to open up Gunter Grove, more as a London *pied-a-terre* than as a home. From there he wrote in 1945: 'I am very sorry that our pleasant arrangement is coming to an end so soon, but I quite understand that with Paul so unwell, and with the many things you will have to do and to think out in connection with the move to your new house [the Rector being forced to retire on health grounds], it will be too much additional burden and responsibility to have the extra worry and work involved by my being at the Rectory over that period. I enclose a cheque for the two weeks ending tomorrow (March 3rd) wh: of course, doesn't include all. . .' Ireland might occasionally haggle over the deduction of a tuppenny stamp, but he was a prompt payer. None could be more genuinely concerned than he for his old friend's worsening heart condition, the main reason for the Waldes taking another house; big enough for Mrs. Walde to augment her husband's small pension with daily pupils and some paying guests, yet more compact than the rambling Rectory, which in any case had to be vacated for a new incumbent.

For a time Ireland remained in Essex, moving in with Gweneth Hutcheson's family. Gweneth was the 'old flame' for whose honour he once called their mutual friend Arnold Bax a cad in musical notation, now settled, unattainable, and a true friend in the maturity of years. His change of address was scarcely a change at all: from Little Sampford (Rectory) to Great Sampford (The White House).

None can better sum up the fascination of several years' close contact between the clergyman's wife and the composer, thrown together by war as they never would have been in peace, than the lady herself. Thus she concluded a letter to the author in 1979, the centenary year of his birth:

'I hope I (have) conveyed to you something of my abiding and affectionate remembrances of a great character, a very hard working and meticulous one. A good and loyal and faithful friend, and one whose impact was considerable upon those who, in one way or another, were brought within its influence. Above all, the affectionate laughter those friends can still enjoy together; of "John doings" and "John sayings" and "John stories"; for always, I'd say, as long as we are here to continue to exchange them.'

As a parting kindness Marjorie Walde agreed that the bachelor musician should send her his underwear for laundering and darning, to conserve the clothing coupons which, even after the war ended, remained more valuable than cash to those concerned with public appearance. 'Send them by post, John' she said. They would be returned after washing and darning to wherever his current abode might be. Eagerly he accepted. She little guessed how great would be her reward for this simple charity; not in heaven, but in the more immediate world of soapsuds, steam, and flat — not 'Slectric' — irons.

In his letters, enclosed in the parcels, socks and sonatas, flimsies and film music, pyjamas and part-songs were discussed as if of equal importance. To a man without a wife, too overworked with commissions to look after himself, they were.

Quotations from a handful of these letters must suffice to recreate the amusement his laundress derived from each parcel of soiled garments: 'I shall bring a fairly hefty lot of socks, and a lot of woollens; I had to *buy* some socks — but they are only six inches long — though very expensive indeed.' Or again: 'Yes, I'm afraid the garments are approaching dissolution. It wld. have occurred long ago but for your skilled and careful attention. Must see later what can be obtained in replacement; only "austerity" I expect.'

Marjorie Walde kept these 'precious garments' going far beyond their allotted span of fibrous life, saving Ireland clothing coupons and cash. In particular, he appreciated conservation work on two fine pairs of silk pyjamas. Parts of a 1945 letter from Great Sampford to Little Sampford are worth quoting as they stand, as a picture both of Ireland the despatcher of unwashed and unmended socks, and of Ireland the man to whom the word 'meticulous' was so often applied both in a musical and a personal sense; so meticulous as carefully to differentiate between feeling *'rather* ill' (underlined once) and *'very* ill' (doubly underlined) instead of merely mentioning some non-fatal everyday malady:

> I am sending you by registered parcel post a few things of the usual sort. I am *very* hard up over the woollies!!
>
> The others not so urgent, as I bought 3 new pairs of socks.
>
> Am still running a temperature, and feel *rather* but not *very* ill. . .
>
> . . . Forgive me sending this parcel at such an inopportune time! Xmas greetings to Paul and yourself,
>
> J.I.

'I laughed and laughed, particularly at "still running a temperature, and feel *rather* but not *very* ill". *Why* is it so funny?' wrote Mrs. Walde to the author, who had returned a large bundle of Ireland's letters to her, inspiring her to re-read it.

Why? Surely because it preserves in only one page the whole spirit of those years of 'John sayings' and 'John doings', and the essence of that hypnotic personality which could make a normally reserved Essex rector talk for hours about 'J.I.', as he would talk about almost nothing and nobody else.

8. The Overlanders

Lean, tough steers herded close together plod across the central right-hand panel of the John Ireland Memorial Window, bringing something of the dry, dusty heat of the burning Australian interior to a cool old London church. They recall Ireland's only excursion into film music, *The Overlanders*, and also the hardest working period of his entire life, when this score overlapped with the overture *Satyricon*, both commissioned to deadline dates, at a time when his health and sight were on the downgrade. Together they nearly broke him, and represent the last major outburst of his life's creative span. After the gruelling late forties, only fairly minor works followed, increasingly spaced out.

Immediate post-war times brought a round of demanding engagements — lucrative, but wearing when executed against the chaotic background of a house and a city putting themselves back into order. Wisely he refused a tempting offer from St. Luke's, Chelsea, to resume his old organist post; inside Ireland the composer was always Ireland the organist, but at present the composer was becoming overburdened. The young Dr. Geoffrey Bush eventually took St. Luke's.

'Excuse haste — am terribly flustered' he ended a pre-Christmas postcard to Marjorie Walde in 1945; 'I have to concoct some talk about Beethoven for "Music Magazine" on December 16th (175th anniversary of his birth!).' How different was his reaction to Beethoven next year when his own *These Things Shall Be* under Sir Adrian Boult ended the final Beethoven night of the first post-war Prom season. Despite the unnerving yet thrilling experience of being pursued down the Prince Consort Steps by a cheering mob of Prommers, which he talked about until 3 o'clock next morning, it was of Beethoven as well as of himself that he was thinking when he added to a remark on Boult's inspired readings, 'I *must* write to him.'

Musicians could no more live at peace in bomb-damaged Chelsea than could greengrocers or bricklayers, when the world was all shortages, strikes, rubble and noise. Life was tough for artist and artisan alike. 'Only a *glimmer* of gas until yesterday' he wrote; 'conditions have been frightful' (here referring to a vicious gas strike). 'Sorry I have not answered you sooner, but life up here is a nightmare,' he continued the sorry saga: '. . . the time seems to go quickly, though full of unpleasant things — such as cold weather, and quite inadequate heating. . . The day I got back here (nearly a fortnight ago) I found a large excavation in the front where it seems there was a leaking water main — which has only just been repaired in a temporary way. To do it properly requires really quite a road engineering job, as it means taking up the pavement and putting in about 25 or 30 feet of new pipe — at *my* expense! Altogether, it is no joke having a house, especially an oldish one, and that well shaken up by bombs, etc.'

Life was not eased when relations with his current tenants-cum-housekeepers became strained. Things worsened once he began to suspect that they had visions of more or less permanent residence. Ireland, 'not renowned for tact' as even his closest associates admitted, thought he could clarify the issue by sending a letter intimating that they should not regard themselves as secure of tenure, or in a home for life. 'Not tactful, but John,' in the words of the one who knew him from semibreves to socks. With the Rev. and Mrs. Walde he spent a 'doleful' 1945 Boxing Day, wondering how much he had offended those who were caring for Gunter Grove, and what the outcome would be. The Waldes themselves were not as cheerful as usual, at an uneasy halfway stage of moving, installed in a rented bungalow until their new home, Howe Hall, was vacated by its uncooperative sellers. 'John, I now remember, did have lunch in that fantastically humble bungalow . . . how quaint it all was, but it was all I could get,' reminisced Marjorie Walde, of yet another slightly unreal period when a celebrated man showed himself perfectly content to throw off fame and be at home under her roof, able to be gloomy without giving offence.

Unsurprisingly the couple, after receiving the letter, began planning their eventual departure.

During this period Ireland, for the first and only time, was lured into writing film music. His eyesight, never strong, was deteriorating, and his health was suspect; but big money was offered for providing *The Overlanders,* in the fashionable spectacular epic format, with background and incidental music. He found himself pursued by producers who were expert in the art of temptation.

Through the war years Ireland's income had undoubtedly dropped. Cancelled concerts, especially in the early years, meant cancelled Performing Rights fees, and the bottom fell out of teaching. Repair bills loomed over damaged Gunter Grove.

Gastric flu seemed to settle the issue. Doctor's orders were to drop work and stay indoors for a week, making discussions and signings impossible. Like unreachable grass the other side of a fence, *The Overlanders* promptly became desirable — a great chance, too good to miss. He liked the star-less plot, featuring huge herds of cattle moving across interminable miles of Australian bush and desert from north to south, driven by rough bushrangers instead of the matinee idols still normally fashionable on the silver screen. The film was complete, shot in Australia itself, needing music tailored exactly by minutes and seconds to fit existing action, underlining anything from the flick of a tail to a terrifying mass stampede.

Disregarding his state of health, Ireland signed up.

Nobody could express better than the man himself the build-up from initial common tiredness to total exhaustion of mind and body, as this project went forward. The whole process can clearly be followed in just three letters. On March 11th, 1946 he wrote to Mrs. Walde:

'I am very much afraid I have at last got "let in" for writing the music for a film. I ignored all their letters, but finally the producer and music director appeared on my doorstep, and browbeat me to such an extent that I had to go back with them and see the film, and practically agree to do the music. They insisted that no-one else could produce the kind of music they want. I have quibbled over the contract as much as I can, but I think they will probably give way on the last point I raised, in which case I shall have to start *at once,* and work at really high pressure for 6 weeks. The pay . . . sounds good, but with 10/- [50p] in the £1 for tax, and the agent's percentage, it is not so very much — but I felt it wld: be foolish to refuse, as I shall probably never get a better chance, as the subject of the film is one I can perhaps tackle, without too much distaste, and the music director will be very helpful, tending my inexperience. But it is a prospect I view with horror, and I felt so ill yesterday that I stayed in bed all day — a slight dose of 'flu, or some germ I think.

However, economically speaking, I felt it wld: be wrong to turn it down offhand — as even the great Vaughan Williams now writes film music. At any rate, I will try it this once — much as I did in the case of that play [*Julius Caesar*]. But this is much more complicated, and it will mean stopping in town all the time and visiting the studios pretty often. . . There is still a *faint* chance that the film will fall through, as I have really been very troublesome to them. I'll write again soon. Meanwhile tell me your news. I shall have to send you a registered parcel with my "undies", I'm afraid — I do hope it won't put you out while you are so busy [moving house]. The laundry here is entirely erratic, and only calls once in 3 weeks.'

Once *The Overlanders* went into full production, Ireland scarcely had time to sleep or eat, let alone think about clean undies. Nevertheless, he found time to send Marjorie Walde a progress report a fortnight later. Already working against the clock, combined with ill-health, is seen taking its toll:

'I have been laid up with gastric 'flu, and have been obliged to have the doctor 3 times — which has seriously curtailed the time available for carrying out the arduous work on this film music. I am getting very interested in it, only I should have liked 6 months, instead of 6 weeks, to do it in.

Of course, I could not *possibly* have undertaken this work without a place of my own in London to work in — and to be available to go down to the film studios at Ealing. . . I shall be condemned to London till the end of April, at least, if not later — but if I can stand up to the work I shall feel I have learned something in a new direction, and an interesting one. Already a second film has been suggested. So, we shall see!'

In the final paragraph, where an ordinary correspondent would simply have wished his friends well in moving house, Ireland embroidered his wishes thus:

'. . . All the best — I will "cross my fingers" and light a votive candle to St. Anthony, on your behalf, in the local R.C. church! I have always found St. Anthony very helpful, believe it or not!!'

He himself leaned towards the High Church (Anglo Catholic) movement. After a quarter of a century of work as an organist he appears to have ceased regular church-going, but always remained a convinced Christian. It could be said that his faith was stated in the impressive church music which is now so firmly established, particularly in his *Te Deum* and the settings known as *Ireland in C* and *Ireland in F*.

In his third letter of the *Overlanders* period Ireland, exhausted from jamming six months' exacting work into only six weeks, plunged straight into a cry of despair:

> 'I am nearly *crazy* with overwork — and nowhere near finished. It's an appalling job . . . I have to broadcast on April 24 (a Wednesday) at 1.15 — have *no time* to practice, either.
>
> I am missing all this fine spring weather, and can only get out of the house for a few minutes daily . . . I can't get to Sampford before May 6 or 7 at the earliest.
>
> Tho' terribly hard, *cruel* work, this film is very interesting and exciting. It is to do with Australia — all about 1000 cattle, horses and drovers, and the obstacles met, in moving the cattle South, when a Jap invasion was expected. It needs a lot of heavy, symphonic music, and what I have done is extremely good and will make an excellent concert suite — but the amount of work is fantastic. I get up at 6 every morning — and work till 1 or 2 a.m. — *every* day!
>
> *TERRIBLE!* . . . Good job I re-established this house — though the expense is simply ruinous. However, this film music will help, although by the time the agent gets his "rake-off" and the tax-gatherer his share there won't be a fortune left. . .'

He ended with a mournful wail for the East Anglian spring there was no time to share: 'The place must be looking lovely — and *I* see nothing but shabby bricks and mortar, alas!'

John Ireland was no globe-trotter, and had never been to Australia. All he had to work on were the silent rushes in the film studio. Yet his music captured the character of the country so convincingly that a native-born Australian composer, with undisguised astonishment, heaped praises upon its 'perfect rightness' and the way in which it caught the very heart of the sun-blistered Outback.

The concert suite mentioned in letters during writing of *The Overlanders* was never produced by Ireland. *The Overlanders Suite*, however, does exist and is one of the most exciting of all modern concert hall items. It was selected and edited after his death by Charles Mackerras, whose talent for realising the music of other composers has been brilliantly demonstrated in several ballets and suites. Five numbers were put together by Mackerras in 1965: a marvellous march, *The Scorched Earth*; a romance, *Mary and the Sailor*; *Open Country*, a very Irelandesque intermezzo; a slashing, almost brutal scherzo, *Brumbies* (portraying unbroken Australian horses); and a finale to set audiences cheering, the hair-raising *Night Stampede*.

Nothing would induce Ireland to go through the rigours of writing cinema music again, even though the film company sent him an open cheque to do Victor Hugo's *Toilers of the Sea*; spoiled for him, in any case, by the addition of a tawdry love plot. He returned the cheque, ending his brief alliance with filmdom. He had rarely written to order in his life; he would rarely do it again. Nor would he use *The Overlanders* material again. It was only as a joke that he occasionally threatened to produce a 'Sinfonia Overlandia' after hearing Vaughan Williams' score for *Scott of the Antarctic* and its companion *Sinfonia Antartica*.

Composing *The Overlanders* to a frantic six-week schedule was sufficient in itself. Combined with an important BBC commission, again racing against time, it made 1946 a killing year.

'You may have wondered why I have not written sooner,' he wrote to Marjorie Walde; 'but the reason is that for the last 6 weeks I have been working excessively hard to complete the new work I foolishly promised for the Prom season. It has been a very tight squeeze, and tho' I have been here [The White House, Great Sampford] nearly 3 weeks I have literally scarcely been outside the house, and working from morning till the small hours daily. In fact, I only finished the score and sent it to the B.B.C. this morning. It has just happened that this year, ever since March, I have had to work much harder than I have ever had to in my life . . . I have to go up to Town soon for a week or two, as I have 3 performances at the Proms between now and September 11 — I had to miss two others as I simply could not spare the time to go up. I am naturally pretty knocked up by all this, and *must* try to avoid a spell like this again, or I shall be in my grave or a lunatic asylum!'

Ireland signed himself wryly, 'Yours distractedly, J.I.'
The cause of this second bout of overwork was the over-

ture *Satyricon*, requested for Sir Henry Wood's 50th Prom season.

Ireland's last major composition, it went wrong from the start, possibly because the composer was too wearied by *The Overlanders* to approach it with his normal affection towards music of literary derivation; in this case, the *Satyricon* of Petronius, in Burnaby's 1694 translation. At one stage he came to a standstill, declaring it 'poor stuff'. Then it began shaping superbly into one of his best orchestral essays. Excitement, as of old, lifted his tired brain from the rut of working to order and back into the joy of working to genuine inspiration. As it now stands, *Satyricon* plunges the listener into the brilliant world of Nero's court of 'licentious pleasures'. Its dazzling orgiastic rhythms are pulled up sharply by the sensuous clarinet interludes written for Frederick Thurston, before careering towards a finale as frenzied as a Roman Saturnalia. Julian Herbage and Anna Instone, presenters for 29 years of *Music Magazine* on radio, received the dedication as an unusual wedding gift.

Who, listening to this electrifying overture, would guess that it was completed in a state of mental and physical exhaustion, due to writing not only *The Overlanders* but also the *Fantasy Sonata* for clarinet and piano (again for Thurston) at the same time?

These three contrasted works comprised his last full-scale spurt of work. 'It has nearly killed me, on top of all that exhausting film work,' Ireland admitted in a letter identifying *Satyricon's* completion date as August 20th, 1946. Even then *Satyricon* was to plague him for two more years; performed from manuscript in 1946, it was not published until 1948.

In spite of being so weary, and by now in his late sixties, he still exerted a power to attract the type of woman who set him retreating as warily as a mouse before a stoat. At *Satyricon's* first-night party he was cornered by as many gushers as true admirers. At another celebration the elderly composer was pounced upon by one described as 'an exotic female'. 'I hear you're on the telephone now, Dr. Ireland,' she purred; 'Can I ring you up?' Ireland spoiled her evening by prevaricating with sham embarrassment and a twinkling eye she did not correctly interpret: 'Er . . . um . . . er, well. . .

Yes . . . Well, I can always disconnect it, can't I?'

Ever conscientious about unwittingly hurting others' feelings — 'a very dear man' as he was once called in a broadcast talk — he anxiously asked an intimate after the butterfly had flitted off seeking easier prey: 'Did I say something I shouldn't?'

He never quite felt at ease with women, or accepted that his sturdy, somewhat masculine writing was suitable for them. Ruth Dyson contributed to this volume an illustration of both points, dating from about 1946:

'. . . two colleagues and I who were then working together as the "New English Trio" presented ourselves at 14 Gunter Grove to play the E-major *Trio* (No 3) to Dr. Ireland, who had promised to put us on the right lines since we were about to perform the work at the Wigmore Hall.

He gave us an excellent coaching on it, but remarked after the Scherzo movement: "You know, the trouble is you ladies are not sufficiently acquainted with the Devil to play my music!"

When I recounted this tale some years later to a well-known pianist who also knew Ireland, he enquired whether the members of the Trio were all women, and on being told that they were, shook his head sadly and said: "Then in any case it would have been a rather terrible afternoon for him." '

The Trio met a memorable example of Ireland's caustic humour which Miss Dyson still treasures. She wrote:

'Another incident that occurred on that afternoon was his lightly pencilled correction of a misreading in my part. He wrote "E-flat, B F". Well, the E certainly needed to be corrected to E-flat, but neither B nor F was present in the chord. It was some time before I realized the letters B and F were not the names of wrong notes but a comment on the intelligence of the pianist. By the time the penny had dropped, it was even too late to laugh.'

Like most people brought into contact with Ireland, Ruth Dyson quickly sensed his almost obsessive feeling of musical neglect, despite the warm tributes which should have reassured him:

'The general impression he made on me was of a very disappointed man . . . but V. W. [Vaughan Williams] was deeply impressed by the E-major *Trio* which we played at an informal series of concerts in Dorking at just about that time, and I believe V.W. wrote an appreciative letter to Ireland about the *Trio*.'

Half a year's toil combined with fullness of years and diminished health began taking a visible toll, worrying to Ireland's many friends. The short and stocky composer who, on good food, good company and plentiful wine, had once jokingly been said to possess almost as many chins as the five lines on a musical stave, and took size 18 collars, was becoming an aging version of the 'whippersnapper' organist of his twenties — almost tiny, thin faced, haggard. Worse was an alarming deterioration in his sight. As far back as 1941 it was clear that spectacles were to him more imperative than gasmarks in wartime, when he wrote to Paul Walde: 'On my arrival (London) I found I had very stupidly left at the Rectory my gasmask; but what is *far* more important, a *grey spectacle case* which contained a pair of glasses without which I cannot read music at the piano.' Urgently he begged for them to be posted back: 'I have to broadcast on Monday and shall be quite helpless without the glasses!' His letter-writing style, incidentally, changed little throughout life, much accentuated — like Queen Victoria's letters — with underlinings and exclamation marks for emphasis.

Signs other than common myopia developed. 'I've got the dazzles' he said to concerned friends, as bright inexplicable lights obscured his vision. They announced the beginning of the end of his career: a composer with fading sight is as deprived as a violinist going deaf, or a crippled dancer.

If ever a man needed a capable wife or housekeeper it was Ireland now, but all he had was the usual succession of factotums, neglectful or even unkind. Some had no appreciation that a musician's fingers, from years at the organ or piano, became as sensitive to the feel of objects as those of a blind man. What did it matter if a cheap Woolworth's spoon lay on his tea saucer instead of one of his beloved silver Georgian ones? To him, it did matter. He was a good cook; too good to enjoy nauseous non-gastronomic odours from boiling bones or cheap fats pervading the house. Ordering a thick green felt door to the basement stairs to be kept closed (Gunter Grove was a typical smaller Edwardian upstairs-downstairs house with a basement kitchen) was no answer. Deliberately the latest cook left it wide open, making her unhappy employer almost physically sick, despairing that his own home was being 'turned into a prison'.

Inviting men into the house — a Victorian blanket-term for a whole range of back-stairs misdemeanours — was a further cause of distress. Sounds of strange male voices in his home almost frightened a sensitive man like Ireland.

Finally he was deserted. Confined to bed with another flu bout, miserable, hungry, burned-out beyond the wish to compose, he was alone when Mrs. Norah Kirby, secretary to the critic and musicologist Ralph Hill, let herself in with the key Ireland had already given her for emergency use. Since being introduced to him by Hill, she had become a most trusted friend.

Woman-like, she set about getting a meal, calling a doctor from a nearby telephone box, and making Ireland comfortable. She left with a promise to call daily while his illness lasted.

Norah Kirby, a widow saddled only with a bombed Putney house, was most free of all those who now call themselves 'The Ireland Family' to help him. He himself suggested she take over the empty ground floor rooms on a trial basis, to see whether they might join forces. 'I like your music,' she told him, but admitted being not a performer. 'I like *you*' he responded, almost naïvely, showing that charming manner described as childlike, but not childish, which enabled him to get on so well with the young. He handed her the ground-floor keys, effectively giving her a separate flat. Each would respect the other's privacy, and live a quite independent life, except for sharing the dining room; but the aging and sick composer would always have someone at hand in case of need.

Her first move on taking fuller charge of Ireland's affairs, without taking charge of his soul — unlike an unsuitable wife or housekeeper — was to pack him off for the holiday he desperately needed to avoid complete breakdown. For once he felt confident about leaving the house in another's charge. He could forget all the quibbling with film producers whose only clear idea of what they wanted was that his music should not sound 'like a Sunday afternoon concert at the Albert Hall'.

To the good Welsh daily help she had engaged to clean and maintain both her own and Ireland's parts of the house, Mrs.

Kirby added an excellent 'daily man to a bachelor gentleman'. Ireland's household was put on a sounder footing than for years.

Once it became clear that they could amicably live in this convenient platonic state, she sold her house and took his lower floor permanently. Except for the declining — but not dead — inspirational side of his life, which she as a music-lover but not a composer could never fully enter, Norah Kirby shared almost everything thereafter: the fireside reminiscences of the past that subtly proclaimed him an aging instead of an active public figure; love of animals, the countryside and Chelsea; drives for pleasure or to the engagements he still attended, usually to hear rather than perform his own music; BBC parties and birthday parties; meetings of lifelong pals; and renewals of war-broken friendships.

Ireland, with increasing help from powerful magnifying lenses, still composed on a smaller scale. Gleams of his natural humour reappeared. He wrote to Marjorie Walde: 'I hope I can come occasionally to Howe Hall, as "The Bevin Boy" ' (compulsory wartime coal miner) after composing what he baldly termed 'my *Coal Piece* which is for mixed chorus and brass band' — a standard colliery town ensemble. He added '. . . received quite a pleasing cheque from the Coal Board for my labours'. *Man in his Labour Rejoiceth* was the Coal Piece's more accurate title. It was suggested by Elisabeth Lutyens and her husband Edward Clark and backed by the National Coal Board. Whether the men, as restive as the workers of today, appreciated this setting of Robert Bridges' stirring lines beginning 'Man, born to toil, in his labour rejoiceth' we are not told.

Automatically Ireland turned to Guernsey for the holiday intended to restore his health. He had not seen it since St. Peter Port vanished over the horizon behind the refugee ship *Antwerp.* Only a few days after the European war ended in 1945 he began thinking about returning, but exiled islanders naturally were given priority on all ferries. A passage was impossible to obtain by a non-native for two years. Dreams of regaining his 'Popish' organist post were dashed when the vicar, preferring a readily available local man to a famous mainlander, intimated that the job was filled. Throughout the war Ireland had dreamed of that relatively humble but satisfying post, as well as of friends left behind.

Autumn was in the air when he, with John Longmire, at last landed in 1947. They were enraptured afresh, 'both quite *carefree*, like boys on a holiday from school'. 'Longmire has "island fever" in a fairly acute form' Ireland reported back to the mainland. Their holiday became a reconnaisance for a new *pied-a-terre*, and a car was ordered in preparation for a return visit in October. Ireland longed to settle in the Channel Islands, to the extent of selling his Chelsea home. But logic told him that though his heart was across the Channel his profession was tied to England. He must always content himself with long visits.

In November he came once more. From the Royal Hotel he enthused: 'The "Island Spell" has got me again, you see...' He stayed to the verge of an unusually early winter: Guernsey had a rare snowfall that year.

His spirits lifted despite finding Fort Saumarez partly wrecked, and beloved Le Catioroc deserted and dreary. He loved the place even in this depressing off-season. 'Yes, I didn't like leaving Guernsey' he confessed in a letter of December 10th, 'but ... it was "work" that brought me back, namely a recital with Peter Pears on December 8th... He is a fine singer, and gave my songs a far better show than they have had since the death of Gervase Elwes.'

The same epistle adds an interesting insight into the state of air travel to the Islands only thirty years ago:

'It began to get cold even in Guernsey about the time I left — there was a pretty good nor'easter the day I flew back. One has to travel *via* Jersey at this time of year, and between Guernsey and Jersey in a small bi-plane (called a *"Rapide"*); the journey was very rough and bumpy. But from Jersey to Northolt was in a Dakota (a 21-seater), which was comfort itself. It is the *only* way to make that journey — 15 mins. Guernsey–Jersey, and 80 mins. Jersey–Northolt. Better than the old way!'

When one door shuts another opens, was one of the favourite maxims of our grandparents. It applied to two of Ireland's more long-standing friendships. For a time, at the end of the decade, Longmire left his immediate circle to work musically abroad, maintaining contact only by correspondence. Fate compensated by bringing back Charles Markes, the ex-St. Luke's chorister whom Ireland had known from 1908 until they parted following a strangely misunderstood encounter in a London street thirty long years ago, after which they had lost sight of each other, as Markes travelled about in showbusiness.

They met again through one of those mundane chances that alter the affairs of men.

'One of our eminent Chelsea residents has just come back to live in Gunter Grove' a voluble local butcher informed Markes as he stood contemplating the limited choice on a post-war counter.

'Oh? Who's that?' responded Markes, without great interest.

'John Ireland.'

Though they had parted seemingly on bad terms and no attempt had been made in three decades to heal the rift, an immediate longing was aroused to see again the man who had meant so much through boyhood and young manhood. He asked the butcher — also Ireland's purveyor — to convey a brief formal message: 'If his housekeeper comes in, ask her to give my regards to John Ireland.' No more than that.

Norah Kirby was surprised by Ireland's reaction when, returning with her meat, she repeated this simple message. The name Markes meant nothing, though she thought she knew all Ireland's friends by now.

Within an hour Charles Markes — living, coincidentally, only a few minutes' walk away in Redcliffe Gardens — received a summons: come at once.

In the old days the two men had nearly always begun their meetings with a half earnest, half friendly altercation on some subject about which they both felt strongly. As the door of Number 14 opened, they instinctively picked up the threads in similar tone and temper. 'Where have you been all these years? I was just going to advertise for you in *The Times*!' barked Ireland. 'It was all your fault! You cut me dead in Great Marlborough Street,' Markes accused Ireland, recalling the rift that had cost them both thirty years of friendship.

'I didn't see you' was the explanation. A few more minutes' talking convinced Markes that Ireland was speaking the truth. Absorbed in musical affairs, and never strong of eyesight, he genuinely had not seen him though their shoulders almost brushed in the crowd. To explain all is to forgive all. The proverb proved very true of these reunited friends. Even Markes' abandonment of classical music for show business, in Ireland's opinion a squandering of the talent he had called 'heaven-born' when Markes was but a child, was tolerated if not condoned. It became another of Ireland's little jokes always to greet his companion: 'Hello, Charlie! What are you doing? Wasting your talent as usual?'

Though slightly deafened by years of close nightly contact with blaring pit trombones and other theatrical uproar, Charles Markes could still recognise anything of Ireland's in a few bars. Before their reunion he and his wife took tickets for a London cinema. They had sat only minutes in the dark before certain harmonic progressions and a characteristic use of the seventh made him exclaim: 'That's by John Ireland.' He was right. The film was *The Overlanders*.

At Markes' home Ireland demonstrated this same aural acuteness, rarely fully developed in non-musicians. An amateur would have shown off at the superb ex-Wigmore Hall grand piano acquired by Mr. Markes, with big chords and spectacular passage-work. Ireland quietly sat down, depressed one low bass note caressingly and softly, judging its muted effect. It told him all about the instrument. 'I'll give you both of mine for it' was his offer.

He was still far from well, plagued by gastric trouble and heart problems, unable to shrug off publishers' demands as easily as before. Two separate publishers, both wanting *Satyricon*, worried him instead of offering a challenge for turning to his own financial advantage, or standing as proof that the neglect he bemoaned was not always true. It took his doctor to see the obvious way out of a problem the depressed composer had magnified out of all proportion — to toss for it. Heads, publisher A; tails, publisher B.

If only sorting out the actual proofs could have been as simple.

Charles Markes, skilled at working on all manner of scores from early Ireland piano pieces to music-hall turns, relieved him of this worst job of his life, when preliminary sheets of *Satyricon* were returned after only sketchy reading.

Markes found a bad mistake on Page One. So many followed that Ireland eventually pleaded, 'Don't look any more — I can't bear it!' Unfortunately some were composer's errors, chargeable against royalties above an allowable maximum. 'This is going to sound like Hell' exclaimed Markes of one section, then discovered that Ireland had forgotten to restore a clef after a transposed passage. Nine more of these mistakes were discovered before the weary creator went off to Guernsey, supposedly to recuperate. Only a few days later a letter arrived, reading 'Everything here is a complete "wash-out", and I hope to return on Friday, when I will get in touch with you and tell you all about it. Meanwhile I understand you have the *Satyricon* proofs, and I shall be interested to know what they are like when we meet.' For once, he was too overwrought to be soothed by Guernsey, tensed up by the problems of preliminary proofs, main proofs, and the whole episode of composing this *Overture* and *The Overlanders* against the calendar. 'I don't know how I kept going,' he confided to Markes; 'I did it on benzedrine and brandy!' Conscientiously, however, he found time to apologise to Mrs. Markes: 'I have monopolized far too much of your husband's time . . . (but) I don't know what I should have done without his help over these music proofs. I could never have straightened them out without his help.' Altogether Markes had discovered over 130 errors.

Yet nobody listening now to brilliant *Satyricon* would dream it was the product of a very tired mind. Its scoring was as original as anything he ever did. While the two men worked together, Markes remarked that whereas a minor composer could find three ways to score a phrase, an experienced musician could think of a dozen, each valid. 'Twenty!' retorted Ireland. He could have made it thirty; not one of them obvious, trite, or anything but Ireland. That was what so fascinated a man with Markes' sensitivity to harmony and accentuation.

When at last *Satyricon* was 'put to bed', in publishers' parlance, Ireland returned neither to Guernsey nor Chelsea, but to the Old Rectory at Ashington in Sussex, where his rented wing was converted into a self-contained flat. He and Arnold Bax, no longer the 'cad' who stole Gweneth, but a good friend, regularly patronised the White Horse at Storrington, Bax's home village, or drove out around the Sussex countryside. Bax, having no car, much appreciated Ireland as the experienced chauffeur he was.

At the end of the fraught forties only a handful of further works left Ireland's pen, none of major importance. One was a setting of the Easter hymn, 'Christ the Lord is Risen Today'. This tune was named *Sampford* after his two happy wartime retreats. Another was his own free arrangement for piano of an attractive forty-year-old organ piece *Villanella*, which had also been arranged for orchestra the previous season, by Ronald Binge. And there was *Columbine,* a single solo contributed to a piano anthology edited by Leonard Isaacs. Only a few isolated phrases were heard coming from the music-room piano before Ireland popped his head out and announced that it was finished. Somewhat ruefully he complained: 'It's turned into a waltz. I didn't mean it to, but it has.' *Columbine,* however, was no conventional ballroom dance; it had simply fallen into triple time of its own accord.

It is sometimes asked whether Ireland followed any special working method in his maturity. Did he habitually compose at the piano? Did he painstakingly revise a phrase several times until it sounded exactly right, or hammer a page into shape bar by bar? The answer to these questions is to be found out of doors instead of in an enclosed music room. Ireland usually composed in his head while walking through some favourite stretch of countryside, notably the Sussex Downs, often at six o'clock in the morning. Entire pages were complete in his mind, ready to be written down when he returned to his cottage or to Chelsea. After playing over only a handful of phrases on the piano he would call for the opinion of Norah Kirby or some other close friend: 'How do you like this?' The movement was complete, never to be altered. Similarly, Ireland furnished his last home 'in his head'. With no plans on paper to remind him of the layout, he directed where each item should go. Again, nothing was changed afterwards.

Another landmark date galloped up apace, Ireland's 70th

birthday. Five years earlier, at Little Sampford, he had amused friends by the umbrage he took at the greater fuss being made of Vaughan Williams at 70, when Ireland was only 65. As they had predicted, now his own 70th was approaching, he had little cause for complaining of neglect. On the contrary, the BBC and other promoters planned to do him proud.

'What's the BBC going to do about my birthday?' he began asking early in 1949. It was intimated that the Corporation, not stopping at a celebration Prom, was contemplating a whole Ireland series. 'Oh, now they're going to kill it off' he answered, almost exactly reproducing his reaction to a previous BBC proposal.

At the 70th birthday Prom his best concert works were played: *A London Overture, The Forgotten Rite,* the *Piano Concerto,* with Eileen Joyce as soloist, and *These Things Shall Be. Epic March,* theoretically the ideal occasional piece, was not included. 'That was a ghastly failure, wasn't it?' was Ireland's own opinion of these pages of hard but less than inspired work, done to order.

Friends and admirers gathering to honour Ireland also renewed acquaintanceship with each other. He was not particularly well, but his capacity for extracting dry amusement from small incidents proved undimmed. Charles Markes never forgot the composer's glee at his own *faux pas* in handing his personal score of the *Piano Concerto* to a famous organist, as requested. 'Don't you want it?' the organist asked politely. '*I* know it' answered Charles, though without intention of insult. He distinctly heared a muffled schoolboyish snigger from Ireland, sitting behind him.

Everybody knew everybody as the 'Ireland Family' and many of the performers gathered afterwards for celebration drinks. The only unfamiliar face was Markes. An eminent colleague finally asked Ireland who was this distinguished-looking figure with the straight actorly bearing. 'Him? Oh, he's one of my choirboys; he's a musician, but I don't understand a note of it' replied Ireland, taking another sly dig at Charles' years on the boards after beginning life singing Mendelssohn and Stanford at St. Luke's. The lady obviously thought him rather beyond choirboy age, adding to Ireland's amusement.

The composer extracted greatest pleasure, during his 70th

year, from a letter intended to insult, antagonise, annoy — anything but make him smile. It came from a butcher with an amateur taste for composition, allied to a flair for vindictive correspondence.

As tampering in the name of exactitude would destroy the spirit which so delighted its recipient, we neither correct his 'London Symphony' into an overture, nor insert any missing capitals:

To John Ireland
Composeur, BBC
London

To John Ireland 'The Great' composer who inflicted Benjamin Britten on the taxpayers of 'Gt. Britten'

Dear Sir

I suppose your works, too, are being subsidised by the british council—

I too know a bit about composition; your London Symphony is the silliest thing I have ever heard! What can one expect from a mediocre englishman?

I suppose you got in with the right set at the right time and since then your "miserable works" have been inflicted on us. I am a butcher and I am afraid that I have to pay towards your pals in the british council

Yours. . . . . . .

P.S. I suppose you are not roman catlik by any chance. I heard that your Benjamin became a catlik recently.

Your London Overture STINKS!

If this letter annoys you I am ready to take up the challenge. I have written more original themes than you but I cannot get them published! All the paper is being wasted on you and Britten and Mr Bliss.

The outraged butcher, far from achieving his purpose, blessed Ireland and his friends with years of laughter. If the scribe should ever see his note here reproduced, it is hoped that in the mellowness of years he will feel pleased rather than angered that Ireland treated it as a treasure, instead of consigning it to oblivion in his waste-paper basket.

9. The Mill

From the opening of the 1950s Ireland's life story becomes personal instead of musical; a progressive physical but not mental decline through which his natural humour still periodically asserts itself, sometimes as mischievous as ever, sometimes almost pathetically wry.

Once turned seventy, age and musical neglect increasingly featured in his correspondence. 'It is alarming that one can so easily pick up something which makes one's life a hell on earth and stops all one's activities — but what can one expect at my time of life?' Ireland addressed Charles Markes, after an infection. At 72 it was: 'Thank you very much for kind letter etc., I received just about the date of my (accursed!) birthday, and for kind greetings to the old wreck'; in 1953: 'Many thanks for your letter and kind greetings — at 73 it should be *condolences,* I think!'; and at 75: 'We old people *must* die.'

Pathos deepened further: 'The "world of music" is no longer any world of mine — my musical days are over — I have no longer any interest in it. Can't believe I used to be a composer!' Thanking Markes for another birthday gift he called himself 'your old friend — rapidly becoming senile'. Ireland took no pleasure in what Boult dubbed 'these melancholy occasions'.

His letters were not all gloom, however. His nonsense verses still not only delighted the recipients, but also those to whom they were almost invariably passed on. One example must here suffice as a specimen of these poetical pranks, appended to a letter to John Longmire. In this he slyly took the mickey out of the latter's teaching-piece *Grasshopper's*

Dance, which Ireland had formerly endured *ad infinitum* when examining:

> Little Beadle, bright and gay,
> Has thrown his "woodlehaf" away —
> No "brodlestonk" or "flonk-a-fellie",
> But trifle-tubs and champagne jellie.

Depression clouded truth when Ireland spoke of having 'no longer any interest' in music. Actually he maintained radio contact with developments to the end, never switching off because another composer's idiom seemed strange. 'He is honest' was his explanation for listening, meaning that he 'had something to say'.

Coupled together, a Hallé Orchestra anecdote and a younger composer's recollections illustrate how Ireland always supported genuine worth — even though he was conscious that the same composer and his contemporaries were turning music away from paths he himself favoured. Waiting at a Cheltenham Festival rehearsal to hear their own works, Ireland and Bax found themselves listening to Barbirolli working on Peter Racine Fricker's *First Symphony.* Ireland turned to Bax, remarking: 'Arnold; there's no room in this world for two emotional old sods like us!' A letter from Fricker himself to the author relates, however, how Ireland once supported him against other adjudicators, exactly as he had supported Britten. For the same reason: obvious talent, worthy of recognition, regardless of the direction it took.

Fricker wrote:

> I did know him a little around 1950 and 1951. By then he was, I suppose, over 70, and I was 30, and just getting started as a composer ... I had heard many stories of his caustic and pessimistic statements about music, his own and other people's (mostly from Humphrey Searle, who, among others, loved him, and delighted to quote him). John Ireland devastated me on one occasion, when a work of mine had won a prize, and had been performed (I think it was the *Concerto for Violin and Small Orchestra,* which was awarded the Arts Council of Great Britain Prize in 1951). Ireland came up to me afterwards and said in his gloomiest voice: "Of course, you know that wouldn't have won the prize if it hadn't been for me — I was on the jury, and nobody else wanted to vote for it."

Depressive phases had always plagued Ireland, when he became convinced of musical neglect. Age intensified these feelings, despite requests for new works from important quarters. For the Festival of Britain the Arts Council suggested another piano concerto; Lady Barbirolli awaited his long-projected oboe sonata; and Sir John Barbirolli hoped for an orchestral work. '. . . Barbirolli is the conductor for my music' Ireland enthused in one paragraph of a 1950 letter; but within ten lines he reverted to disillusionment: 'He wants me to do a new work for him for 1951 — but whether I can write any *more* music, I do not know. Is it worth the "fag"???' As he was still capable of driving excellently, his sight was not yet too poor for composition, though it was a strain. Seventy-phobia — depression rooted in the calendar — seems to have destroyed his will. Yet humour, ingrained into his makeup, rescued him from self-pity. It bubbled up even in the BBC studio where *This Week's Composer* went out daily for many years. Asked how he enjoyed being joint composer of the week with Holst he twinkled spontaneously: 'H'm . . . very nice — but there's rather a lot of up-HOLST-ery with it.'

Finance worried him, particularly taxation. 'I have been studying the new Budget and enclose the official figures of how you will be affected' he addressed Charles Markes; 'a warning to you not to make *too much* money! In other words, not to work too hard . . . I warn you that music is a very severe strain on one's eyesight, which you should consider before the damage is done.' In another epistle he exclaimed: '. . . we have both chosen a rotten profession, where success only comes to those who blow their own trumpets, *fff,* continuously.'

'Why on earth can't they take all my cheques, help themselves, and send me back what is left over?' he exploded once to Norah Kirby, bothered as usual by his accountant's imminent arrival.

'Well, you know, I'm an old fogey; musical fashions change like women's clothes. There may come a time when my income will drop. What are we going to do?' he pondered. Somebody once, unkindly, called him 'the most glorious pessimist I ever knew'; but Ireland was also a realist, visualising decreasing royalties from decreasing compositions. 'I'm not worried, but if I'm going to have trouble I like to know, so I can be prepared to deal with it when it comes', was his creed. With a flash of old fire he added: 'If somebody's going to stab you, it's no good waiting till the knife is in your back.'

Biggest of his post-war concerns was the destruction of old Chelsea by noise, fumes, ugliness, and lorries thundering day and night through once-dignified Gunter Grove. Graphic descriptions of pandemonium's rape of his road went to friends. This passage, to Mrs. Walde, typifies them:

> '. . . here I am driven nearly out of my senses by continuous heavy lorry traffic in this once *quiet* street. All the residents are up in arms about it, the houses are being shaken to pieces, and life here is almost intolerable for elderly people who cannot go out much, like myself . . . London has changed greatly during the last few years, and I feel the time has come for me to leave it, if possible, and arrange to live out my last chapter in the country. There is really nothing to keep me here any longer. Chelsea, as it used to be, no longer exists, and one feels like a *ghost* here, with every trace of the old associations vanished.'

He retreated more frequently to Ashington, alternately rhapsodising over Sussex's peacefulness and bemoaning its cost. 'The question of those rooms at Ashington is not free from snags, but what else could I do?' he asked John Longmire; 'I must have somewhere to escape to, away from London and in the country, and where I can be on my own, and do whatever I fancy. In a guest-house that is impossible. . . And it just happened that I could have those three small rooms at Ashington, quite cut off from the rest, like a small flat — *with* attendance on the premises, and meals — not *good* meals, but still, something. And it is not cheap — but I ask you, what *is* cheap these days? . . . I am having to put in a bath etc., at my own expense, and have the place decorated — but this will cost very much less than buying a cottage (*if* one could find one) and setting it in order — *and* paying and supporting a housekeeper (*if* one could find one). . .'

Sussex interludes emphasised London's insanity, strengthening his resolve to cut his ties of fifty years, could the right house be found. Only one city sound now afforded him entertainment instead of distress; a battalion of feral cats, bombed-out refugees. Always a cat lover, he treated them like naughty but intelligent children. 'Now *stop* it' he ordered when a specially savage fight erupted outside Norah Kirby's window. Flinging wider his own, on the top floor, he lectured them thoroughly: 'I won't *have* it, d'you understand? I don't want to throw water over you, but you're disturbing the whole neighbourhood — I won't *have* it.' The soaking brought louder indignant yowls. '*Now* perhaps you'll go away.' Slam. Silence.

Drenching fighting toms worried him more afterwards than it did the animals.

In 1953 the young Elizabeth II was crowned. In her honour leading British composers devised the choral anthology *A Garland for the Queen,* each contributing one piece. *The Hills,* unaccompanied, was Ireland's offering, among his last compositions.

Sir Arnold Bax, Master of the Queen's Musick, died during Coronation year. The composer's letter to Charles Markes is saddening; whoever will be next Master, he realises, it will not be Ireland:

> Bax's sudden death came as a great shock, so soon after Quilter. Bax was not yet 70, and I used to envy him his health, good appetite and powers of getting about. Well, well. I wonder who will now be "Master of the Queen's Musick"? Perhaps Walton or Britten. The world of music knows *me* no more. I am as much a "back number" as Holbrooke, Cyril Scott, and Bantock. Well, every dog has his day. Mine is over.'

Ireland and Bax had always been wary friends. He was bitterly hurt when Bax — with power over the Honours List — casually remarked: 'I haven't put you up for an honour, old man, as I know you don't like that sort of thing.' Ireland, though modest, would have appreciated being given formal opportunity to refuse — or accept.

He was contradictory even about honesty. Guiltily he once apologised to Paul Walde for accidentally taking his Japanese stick home. Now (1953) he was horrified, on turning out a lumber room, to discover an item abstracted unintentionally eight years ago: 'I was astonished — *and shocked* — to find in an old tea-caddy a beautiful silver tea-measuring spoon which I at once recognised as belonging to *you*!' . . . I had no *idea* I had it — you must have missed it. It is valuable, and probably an heirloom of yours.' Hastily he put it into the registered post. Yet one of his favourite treasures, impishly displayed, he openly admitted was not his, a cheap ordinary india-rubber: 'I stole it from a girls' school where I was examining' he often crowed. 'He seemed proud of this feat, and probably valued the rubber more than if it had been presented to him, though any headmistress would have been proud to give it, if she had been asked' commented Marjorie Walde.

Coronation year brought Ireland a thing he had coveted for thirty years; his dream home, discovered whilst weekend-ing at Ashington, with Norah Kirby installed at a nearby cafe/guest house. Driving back from browsing around Steyn-ing's charming antique shops, a favourite relaxation, they one day passed Rock Mill at Washington, a windmill converted into a comfortable home which he had long admired. By Coronation Day a house agent's board had appeared: FOR SALE, it read. Mrs. Kirby was departing to tour Normandy and Brittany next day, during which 'J I' would inspect the mill. Mrs Kirby had scarcely booked into a Dieppe hotel be-fore, with excitable Gallic gesturing, she was handed an Ex-press Delivery letter from Ireland. Rock Mill 'made every other house we have looked at seem a slum' he enthused: they had visited many around Chanctonbury Ring.

The sellers found Ireland easy to deal with. They, in turn, were co-operative and businesslike. Through Ireland's solicitor the deal was clinched.

An urgent message to Mrs. Kirby — 'I can't run this place without you' — settled her position. Within three months they were installed, she in her own independent quarters yet always within reach, as at Chelsea.

Ireland's most peaceful years had begun despite the spectres of age, failing sight and fear of musical neglect. Mrs. Kirby's pretty half-Siamese black cat, Tigger, joined them. Their hearth, as well as their home, was complete.

'It was a very drastic step to take at my age' Ireland con-fided to Charles Markes, still living in Chelsea, 'but I think it was the right one. Yesterday I had a long letter from the Town Clerk of Chelsea from which it is perfectly clear that NO steps will be taken to diminish the traffic in Gunter

Grove, in spite of our petitions, etc. Had I still been living at No. 14 I should really have been in despair. . .'

Friends received happy letters, like this to Markes:

'. . . It would be difficult to describe this place to you. It is wonderful and absolutely unique. . . There is a wonderful music room, the lowest room of the windmill, octagonal in shape, large and lofty with walls 3 feet in thickness. The rest of the accommodation was built by the previous owner, regardless of cost. . .'

Soon, however, restlessness overtook Ireland. Country life had soothed him for weekends; permanent peace, without familiar London sounds, became almost unnerving. A well-meant gift of a book on Old Chelsea brought his misgivings into the open. He was homesick for noisy Chelsea.

Norah Kirby applied psychology to the problem. After driving him to London she parked at 14 Gunter Grove and kept him sitting for half an hour outside his former house, deafened by roaring lorries. Then she took him back to Sussex. He never pined for Chelsea again.

His letters returned to rapture. 'This place is *quite different* from anything you have ever seen, or could even imagine!' he told Charles Markes; 'At first, and for some months, I felt miserable here, after living 60 years in London streets (and sordid ones, at that). However, all that is now changed, and I would not dream of living anywhere else — in fact it is a pain to leave Rock Mill even for 24 hours! You must come here at the earliest possible moment. . .' He repeated this invitation to Charles frequently.

Under the doorbell was screwed his distinctive plaque; not reading 'Ring' but, in capitals, 'AEQUANIMITAS': equanimity; composure; mental tranquillity.

Of all Ireland's homes and *pieds-a-terre* — in Chelsea, Ashington, Eastergate, Deal, the Channel Islands, Great and Little Sampford — the last was his most loved. Rock Mill appears to the right of his portrait in his memorial window, with its little high balcony where the sails once fanned out. Like the other panels, this is a study in blues: a fitting colour for the Sussex windmill where his life's evening darkened into dusk.

At first Ireland continued driving. A motorist for half a

century, he had immense experience but no time for modernity. 'Have you still got your nice Morris which has served you so well? I have an Austin 8 wh: I bought in 1949 and shall stick to. I *detest* all these new cars with grinning fronts in American style, tho' no doubt they are considerably faster than mine . . .' he wrote to Mrs. Walde. This car, bought in Guernsey, replaced one left behind in fleeing the Nazis. At 75 he still drove. After celebrating that landmark birthday at a Steyning inn, Ireland was the only one sober enough, after a specially potent perry laced with brandy, to take his friends back to the Mill. At the foot of a steep hill he accelerated, when suddenly a cyclist shot from a side turning, overturned, and fell into his path. Someone shouted to slam on the brakes, but with a lightning twist of the wheel Ireland slipped round man and bicycle, without touching either. 'H'm . . . I might have killed that man, mightn't I?' he mused. Nothing ruffled Ireland on the road.

The 75th birthday itself meant the usual celebration Prom, under Sargent, with the *Piano Concerto* and *These Things.*

Ireland retained his interest in newer composers, particularly his ex-pupil, Britten. 'I have listened twice to Britten's new opera "The Turn of the Screw" ' he told Markes in 1954; 'I am no judge of opera as such, but this contains the most remarkable and original music I have ever heard from the pen of a British composer — and it is on a firmly *diatonic* and *tonal* basis. Also, what he has accomplished in sound by the use of only 13 instruments was, to me, inexplicable; almost miraculous. This is not to say I *liked* the music, but it is gripping, vital, and often terrifying. I now am (perhaps *reluctantly*) compelled to regard Britten as possessing ten times the musical talent, intuition and ability of all other living British composers put together.' It seemed an eternity since the schoolboy Britten had walked into an audition with his cap on the back of his head and dumped a score before Ireland and his two fellow adjudicators. 'It isn't decent for a boy of his age to be writing this sort of music' Vaughan Williams had remarked. Such departures were *not* decent in 1930; but they were genius.

Ireland now visited London only when his own works were played. 'London is now quite impossible with the enormous traffic and the horrible fumes emitted from buses, lorries and other vehicles which use Diesel oil, and I am thankful to be out of it' he concluded.

Wisely he registered with a local doctor. He wrote to Markes, after remarking with pleasure that Longmire and his wife had returned from New Zealand: 'I had occasion yesterday to call in a doctor (nothing very serious) and I got one who has a good local reputation. He is an Aberdeen man . . . and I rather liked him.' The Steyning chiropodist pleased him less, by asking a heavier fee for going out specially to Rock Mill. 'Don't forget to let me know when you're going to someone else in future' he instructed; 'All these little things count, you know!' The chiropodist laughed, but took the hint.

Age was mentioned ever more frequently in his letters. 'I have lived many years too long. When one's faculties deteriorate (as they *do*, progressively) one becomes a nuisance to oneself and a burden to others' he reminded the younger Charles Markes; 'In a civilized country there should be voluntary euthanasia for anyone over 70. One gets too old and tired to continue the struggle.'

Pathetically he once asked Markes: 'When are you coming down to see the old composer who is now decomposing?'

Markes' summer Blackpool season ('I hope the job was a well-paid one! and in cash!!') revived memories: 'I was taken there as a child in 1885, that is, 71 years ago! Later I did some adjudication at the Competition Festival, about 1930. . .' Ireland thought again of his Bowdon and Manchester upbringing. To Barbirolli ('My very dear John') he confessed '. . . both I and my origins are especially Mancunian, of which I am proud.'

To Paul Walde he wrote '. . . (the) days when you and I were both at St. Luke's . . . seem a long way off. Quite another world . . . most of its occupants are dead.'

Content with Sussex, he even stopped talking of Guernsey.

Painful dental troubles were Ireland's next problem. 'He had the worst teeth I ever saw,' Mr. Markes told the author. He was always reluctant to face dentistry, until an 'accursed germ' from decaying molars made his mouth agonising and smoking impossible. Surgery was his punishment, described in several letters. Here he regales Marjorie Walde with his 'drastic dental operations':

> '. . . on September 11 I went into a London nursing home and had the thing done properly and in comfort — by first-rate people. It was well worth the expense, for I knew absolutely nothing about it, and no pain afterwards. They have brought anaesthetics to a fine art now. . . When I "came to" about 6 hours later I simply did not believe it when the nurse said "*it is all over!*" I was not even aware that I had left my bed at all. Quite astonishing. . .'

Ireland was not as deaf as he imagined, except to high frequencies, like most elderly people. This a leading pianist discovered when visiting Sussex for discussions. 'I'm afraid I can't do much to help you' Ireland apologised, leaning over the piano; 'I'm a very old man; I'm nearly blind, and I'm deaf.'

The soloist struck one chord. Ireland jerked alert:

'*What* was that you played? That wasn't one of *my* chords.'

The visitor played it again.

'You didn't play that the first time.'

On leaving the pianist commented: 'I say this in all reverence; if ever I have to play to a composer who is *not* deaf, then God help me!'

Visitors included critics as well as performers and composers, in particular Scott Goddard of the now defunct *News Chronicle*. Ireland also maintained friendly relationships with William Mann of *The Times,* Feruccio Bonavia (*Daily Telegraph*) and Ralph Hill (*Daily Mail*).

Age was a time for fireside reminiscences with Norah Kirby or visitors:

— of slyly taxing Sir Arthur Bliss: 'H'm . . . not a bad thing, being Master of the King's Musick. At least it ensures you get plenty of performances of your own music,' and countering Bliss' denial of hogging broadcasting time with: 'How singularly unsuccessful his efforts appear to be!'

— of Gershwin asking: 'Doctor Ireland, I hear you've written a *Rhapsody*; how many performances does it get a year?' Three, Ireland honestly confessed. 'Ah! *Mine* gets played two or three times a *day*!' 'Gershwin's a genius in some ways' Ireland had admitted, starting *The Man I*

Love on Charles Markes' piano. 'Gershwin wouldn't play it like that' — Markes demonstrated in experienced, embellished theatrical style. 'You're making that up!' Ireland retorted.

— or of hearing Brahms' *First Symphony* premiered under the legendary Nikisch. Often now he disappeared for an hour and returned happy, saying to Mrs. Kirby: 'I wish you'd been with me to hear Nikisch conduct the *C-minor Symphony.*' He had heard it right through — in his mind's ear.

Ireland grew increasingly old-fashioned and courtly. Most people were addressed as Miss. . . . . . ., Mrs. . . . . . ., or Mr. . . . . . . Only in true intimacy did he use Christian names, and rarely diminutives. He was Dr. Ireland to all but close friends, but even one of these admits sometimes instinctively calling him Sir. Mildly objectionable language was reprimanded. 'Now, . . ., you seem to forget that Norah is in the room, and I can't have that sort of thing in front of a lady' he once scolded, though alone with men he spoke men's language. He recognised no ill, and eschewed professional jealousy. 'You shouldn't say that; you make me feel very angry' he cautioned someone alleging that another musician was no friend to him.

He loved College students coming to play his music at Rock Mill. Children were fascinated by his old-world custom of bowing and shaking hands with small boys. Visiting musicians' little girls curtsied. '*Must* we go? Can't we come and live with that darling old gentleman?' one child pleaded. Another followed him when he went for his afternoon nap, crying 'Where is he?' Cautiously she opened his bedroom door, catching him with his hair over his face, brush in hand, and Smokey the cat on the bed. 'What's this?' he exclaimed, kindly enough, before having her removed to avoid disturbing Smokey's sleep, rather than his own.

In 1958 he was tempted into a swan-song, *Meditation on John Keble's Rogationtide Hymn.* This profitable American commission drew him back to his favourite instrument. 'I've *concocted* a piece for organ' he informed Charles Markes, asking his help as amanuensis. Laboriously *Meditation* was handwritten, with a powerful magnifying glass covered with

144

yellow cellophane to intensify the image held in his left hand. Markes relieved him of making two further required copies. At the Mill, Ireland held the sheets under a white floodlight, additional to blazing summer sunshine. 'I can't see the lines or spaces' he whispered sadly. Between laboriously 'concocting' *Meditation* and checking the copies, he had become virtually blind.

Gently Markes guided his hand to insert one missing accidental in his own writing. Ireland twice asked to pay his old friend (Charles in speech, still the boyish Charlie in letters) at 'the proper rate'. Of course Charles refused, considering the honour of Ireland's trustfulness enough. 'He was pathetically grateful for anything you did for him,' he recalled, including 'bringing to its senses' a temperamental grandfather clock with which Markes had a knack.

Meditation brought Ireland's career full circle. It ended as his first major work began; with the soft, mystic, beautiful chords introducing *The Forgotten Rite*.

Did he realise it? Or consciously think, my beginning is now my end?

These were the last notes ever penned by John Ireland, composer.

A Brighton ophthalmologist's remark, 'Many people would give all they possessed to have what sight you still have left', deeply distressed him. Undoubtedly it was true; but as a composer, dependent upon writing, he was under a death sentence.

All the same, he managed for a while to undertake a few assignments. When a prominent journal sent a new biography of Barbirolli to be reviewed by a man of similar professional stature — Ireland — he gladly undertook laboriously to study it. 'I was given the pleasant task of reviewing (for *Musical Times*) C B Rees' book on yourself and the Hallé' he wrote to the conductor; 'I hope you see this, as it gave me the opportunity of expressing publicly my devotion and admiration for you and your unique genius.'

Visitors and Mrs. Kirby's cat were his comforts, but black Tigger from Chelsea died at seventeen, on Ireland's 80th birthday eve. 'Shall we ever be happy again?' he moaned at a catless fireside. Another pet was the answer.

Five Siamese kittens were brought to him. 'How can I choose, when they are all so adorable?' he exclaimed, meeting five pairs of mischievous sapphire eyes. Standard cat technique was applied: let them choose for themselves. Ireland sat down. Immediately one little queen (female) clambered onto his knee and shoulder, purring into his ear. 'There's your cat. She's sold herself' the breeder confirmed. 'Her blue eyes look at me through a haze of smoke' Ireland noticed, as her eyes and seal points — ears, tail, paws, mask — darkened. 'I shall call her Smokey.' He could just see those blue optics, if very close.

When his sight finally failed, affected by an arterial condition, Smokey — always near, usually sleeping on his bed — partially compensated for the lost pleasures of reading and driving himself.

He still enjoyed country drives with others. Once, at Shipley churchyard, a handsome prowling ginger tom delightedly responded to Ireland's tickling behind the ears. Thereafter they met frequently, composer and cat sitting contentedly together outdoors, enjoying the Sussex sunshine. Soon Ginger knew the sound of the car engine, and came trotting straight out with tail in air. Ireland's answer to 'Where shall we go?' became predictable: 'Let us go to Shipley and see that delightful cat.'

Ireland became music's first patron of the Crusade against all Cruelty to Animals, hoping that others would follow. A dozen did, including Yehudi Menuhin.

His 80th birthday was commemorated at the Proms, though Tigger's demise the previous evening blended sorrow into his pleasure. Ailing, he did not attend personally, but Sargent and the BBCSO honoured him with affectionate performances of *The Forgotten Rite*, the *Piano Concerto*, and *Satyricon*.

In tribute, *A London Overture* inaugurated the entire season. Ireland appeared on stage; aged, thin, tiny, accepting thunderous applause.

Youth paid its own homage. A student group formed the John Ireland Society (now disbanded) for promotion, preservation and performance of his works.

Surely there was no reason now to feel neglected?

Only one season later Ireland bitterly told Charles Markes: 'They have kicked me out of the Proms this year.'

Yet Ireland accepted age, disabilities and a changing world with philosophical resignation. Such close friends as Anna Instone and Julian Herbage, visiting the Mill towards the end, marvelled at his uncomplaining attitude towards the near-blindness which deprived him of reading, letter-writing and composition, and made his beloved Downs and garden only a dim, blurred outline.

'You mustn't be sorry for me' he reproved Norah Kirby when she sympathised; 'I'm over eighty; I have no pain; I have Smokey, and you, and this lovely home, and live in this glorious Downland. I am a very lucky man.' His nearest approach to outright complaint was: 'It's a mistake to live to eighty, you know.'

Soon this quiet finale to his symphony of life would reach its inevitable coda.

10. Quiet Sleep and a Sweet Dream

Scarcely two years of quiet decline were now left to John Ireland. His sight and health continued to deteriorate, but mentally he remained alert.

Carefully he listened to broadcasts of new works, more keen to commend than to destroy. Mere 'note-spinning' without genuine sensitivity he detested, but still listened to the bitter end if a modern composer was 'honest', having something worthwhile to say, even though Ireland admitted hating the actual sounds, and sometimes exclaimed: 'I despair of the path music is taking.'

Abandonment of beauty in much contemporary music seemed to emphasise how old-fashioned were his personal values in melody, harmony and expressiveness. This brash new generation appeared to have no place for an 'emotional old sod'.

Ireland felt himself a forgotten man as his works were less frequently played.

Nevertheless he felt reasonably satisfied with his output. Replying to the young Canadian composer Murray Schafer during an interview he said: 'I've not written a great many large scale works, but I've always written what I wanted to write, when I had something to say, and have always tried to express myself sincerely.'

An ending of earthly life must now be faced. Because making a will forces acknowledgement of man's mortality, many fail to do so. Ireland was no exception until two close friends, independently of each other, tackled him on Mrs. Kirby's future. She had given sixteen years to caring for him, his affairs and his home; her position should be assured, apart from other legacies. He took the easy solution of leaving all to her;

Rock Mill, its contents, his royalties and assets. Otherwise all would have gone, under a thirty-year-old will, to the dedicatee of *On a Birthday Morning*. Since Ireland's death this money has been treated as a trust rather than personal assets, used to establish the Memorial House, to underwrite posthumous publication of unpublished works, and to commission memorials and recordings.

Among Ireland's final musical experiences was a concert marking his 82nd birthday, at which Sir Arthur Bliss asked leave to 'stress the man's generosity' as well as his achievements; but one night of honour could not dispel his belief that the wider world ignored him. 'He rarely complained, but he was suffering inside,' as Charles Markes said.

In other ways Ireland could call himself fortunate, surrounded by friends who counted the humblest service an honour, and with a doctor who willingly came day or night from Angmering to the Mill. Medicine, however, could only ease time's march, not halt it. Bronchial and gastric problems and a weakening heart combined with further fading of his sight, although his hearing remained fairly good, apart from high-pitched sounds and very soft unfamiliar voices; friends had no need to shout. He conversed less and thought more, walked increasingly slowly and looked more frail, but country drives and meetings with his 'delightful cat' at Shipley churchyard continued. His appetite almost died. Norah Kirby and other friends often drove to Worthing for tempting delicacies, but after a few mouthfuls of salmon or best plaice he apologised, 'I'm sorry; I can't eat any more.' He did appreciate a bottle of champagne from Charles Markes. 'No, Sir; I brought that down to do you good,' Charles replied to his invitation to share it; the old choirboyish Sir still resurrected itself sometimes, after half a century. Ireland went off to his room, cuddling the bottle like a baby.

Smokey the Siamese was his unfailing comfort. She could do no wrong. When she leapt onto an antique table, sending flying a treasured set of Chelsea ware, he only said: 'Oh, Smokey, you *are* a naughty little girl. You *know* I love that china.' He was too blind to realise how tiny were the fragments Mrs. Kirby retrieved and glued together like a porcelain jigsaw. This lovely set is now displayed at Steyning, cunningly placed to disguise the glued cracks. She seemed to sense that her master was failing, joining Norah Kirby every evening as she helped Ireland upstairs and along the corridor to his room. Not until the door was loudly and convincingly closed and she was told, 'There, Smokey, he's safely in', would the young cat rest. Often she spent the night on his bed.

Many visitors came to the Mill, each conscious that this was probably the last time he would meet a loved friend. Some were famous, such as Sir Arthur Bliss, Sir Eugene Goossens, Norman deMuth, Dr. Geoffrey Bush, Dr. Alan Bush, William Alwyn, and William Wordsworth. Percy Turnbull and his wife came down several times. Whilst Mrs. Turnbull and Mrs. Kirby chatted, the two musicians — master and pupil turned friends — retired into private talk of music and other topics, enclosed in Ireland's sitting room, until a call to tea made the visit more generalised. Charles Markes, the chorister who first met Ireland before the Great War, was among the last to see him. 'Norah; shall I ever see Charlie . . .' came the familiar voice as Markes walked away down the corridor. He never heard the final word, 'again'. Among Ireland's last requests to Mrs. Kirby was: 'Don't lose touch with Charlie Markes.' She never did.

John Longmire came whenever examining tours allowed, having his own room at Rock Mill.

Probably the last outside visitor was Marjorie Walde, his wartime hostess, who arrived only a fortnight before his death. It was a glorious May day, but his bedroom was darkened. Despite warnings, she was shocked by his appearance; yet his mind was bright, and his thoughts all of former Little Sampford friends, even the humblest. When she mentioned an Ireland song to be used at a schools' festival and asked his preferred tempo, he promptly sang it right through, beating time on the sheets. 'Well, goodbye, my dear. Come and see me again' he said as she left. To his face she replied, 'Yes, I will'; but downstairs she told Norah Kirby 'I have said Goodbye to John.'

Recounting her memories, Mrs. Walde said: 'That is my final memory; but not the one I think of most often; it is rather of all the laughter' — the laughter of those wartime years when the composer shared her home and kitchen.

Ireland long nursed a strange conviction that he would 'end life very impoverished' and in 'mean surroundings', probably rooted in childhood insecurity. 'I shall live till I'm 81 — a fortune teller told me' he added to intimate friends. In the event he died at 82, in a place far removed from poverty or meanness; at his lovely home, Rock Mill. On June 12th, 1962, he breathed his last. Heart failure was given as the principal cause of death.

To quote the closing words of his famous song *Sea Fever*, the time had come for drifting into '. . . quiet sleep and a sweet dream, when the long trick's over.' His music to that sensitive phrase by Masefield now curves, in the shape of a rainbow, across the top of his memorial window in London.

When the question of his resting place was discussed, those closest to Ireland could think of no more appropriate spot than the churchyard of the 'delightful cat' where some of the most placid hours of his old age had been spent. He is therefore almost certainly the only major composer whose last home was chosen not for its pomp or its associations with the famous, but because of a humble ginger tom.

To Shipley he was taken on June 16th, a blazing summer day. The church was filled with as many unpretentious but devoted friends as famous names. Inside, the organist played solemn music. Outside, the songs of birds made the Sussex Ireland loved joyful instead of sad.

11. The Window

The period following Ireland's death was a time for gratitude as well as for mourning: for tangibly recognising his stature as man and musician. This gratitude was expressed in the monuments erected in three parts of England specially closely associated with him.

To the dedicated persistence of Stuart Scott, then a student at the Royal Manchester College of Music, Bowdon in Cheshire owes a commemorative plaque erected by the local council, identifying 'Inglewood' in St. Margaret's Road as Ireland's birthplace. Unlike London's blue discs fixed to the walls of famous men's former homes, this distinguished-looking bronze inscription is attached to the gate-post.

Inside Shipley church in Sussex another plaque was installed, to direct visitors to the unusual monument standing sentinel over his grave in the churchyard. It was designed by the Sussex sculptor John Skelton and reads '. . . his resting place opposite the south door of this church is marked by prehistoric Sarsen stones to symbolise that antiquity the love of which inspired much of his music.'

The most impressive and best known tribute to the composer is the John Ireland Memorial Window erected in 1963 in the Musicians' Chapel of the Church of the Holy Sepulchre in London. It was designed by Brian Thomas (creator also of the Melba window) from ideas roughly sketched out by Norah Kirby.

This memorial window was formally unveiled at noon on 22nd November, 1963 — St. Cecilia's Day, music's patronal festival. In addition to the cameo portrait of Ireland and the panels illustrating Chelsea and the Channel Islands, Maiden Castle and Rock Mill, *The Holy Boy* and *The Overlanders*, it

152

shows the figure of St. John the Divine sitting on a rock with an eagle beside him, gazing towards his Revelation vision of the New Jerusalem. It is specially appropriate that St. John should be Ireland's name-saint, as he is called the prototype of inspiration.

This was also a period to regret the loss of the music Ireland might have written had all his ideas come to fruition, and had not diminishing sight and disappointment in the post-war musical world combined to reduce his will to compose. 'The Press critics have no use for music which they suspect of . . . being "romantic". It is anathema to them!' Ireland commented to Lady Barbirolli ten years before his death. He had long thought of writing something specially for her. '. . . He really did contemplate an oboe work with strings, which of course — sadly — he never wrote — we had quite a correspondence about this. . .' Lady Barbirolli confirmed to the present writer. 'I felt I must write and tell you how much I enjoyed your performance (over the air) of the Strauss Concerto the other evening' Ireland wrote enthusiastically to Lady Barbirolli as early as 1950; '. . . till your performance I had no idea what a delightful work it is, and how effective. In your hands the oboe part showed a range of feeling and style which, to me, was quite unique, and made one feel one might even have a shot at something for oboe and orchestra oneself. Also, I was more than thankful to hear once more the *true* oboe quality, which in recent years has, for me at any rate, been conspicuous by its absence. You must remember I knew the oboe before it became the fashion to make it sound like a fiddle!!' Three years later Ireland dropped another hint, suggesting how the instrument might sound to advantage with strings alone: 'I saw Capell's notice of the Gardner sonata, which must have owed much to its performance by such a consummate artist as yourself . . . Personally, I feel that the oboe is heard to greater advantage with strings, than with the piano. Were I to write for the oboe, it would be with strings, I think.'

What lush spread of rich orchestral sound was in mind when Ireland spoke of tailoring a work for the Hallé Orchestra and Barbirolli? A tantalising hint appears in his 1950 letter to Lady Barbirolli:

'I hope you and John are well and not too overworked. Now there are two things I want you to tell John. First, I hope to come to the Cheltenham Festival for my "Satyricon", and I am anxious to know when his rehearsal there will be, so that I can come to it (date and time). Then, I have been seriously considering the question of a new work, *for him*, in 1951, and though I have not yet a note on paper I have, at least, the glimmering of an idea, which, with luck (and crossed fingers) I hope and pray may turn into something tangible. A first performance by John is indeed something to inspire one to write something worthy of his mettle. (But "mum's the word" at present, in case I fail.)'

Sir John Barbirolli, as guidance to his wife when answering this letter, wrote across the top: 'Tell him publishers have agreed to keep a set of Satyricon entirely for my own use' (Ireland had offered a manuscript set of parts on permanent loan, to 'frustrate that troublesome young man who is running - - - - - - - - - - Ltd'). Barbirolli added: 'reh. July 6 between 10–1', and the delighted comment 'Thrilled at possibility (of) a new work.'

That thrill was denied to the world at large, as well as to Barbirolli.

On the other hand, some previously unknown Ireland works were published posthumously, reviving a controversy which often follows the death of a composer — to publish or not? One school of thought insists that a composer who suppresses work knows what he is doing, and probably considers it sub-standard: another believes that the public has a right to know his entire output and to judge for itself. Ireland's executor favoured the second view. Among these posthumous pieces were the *Ballade of London Nights,* considered by its composer to be inferior to the larger *Ballade* ('It didn't quite come off, did it?', he confessed to Charles Markes) and *Vexilla Regis,* an unrevised early *Hymn for Passion Sunday,* of which Stanford had thought so highly as to arrange a performance at Holy Trinity, Sloane Street. *Vexilla Regis,* written when Ireland was only nineteen, is a remarkable work for choir, organ and brass ensemble which has recently been recorded for the first time.

Eventually Rock Mill was sold, but the contents were transferred to Norah Kirby's new home, the John Ireland Memorial House in the attractive old High Street at Steyning, a village the composer loved. 'Aequanimitas' was screwed back beneath the doorbell. The rooms were arranged as close replicas of those at the Mill, notably the Chelsea Room (dining room) and the Music Room.

In the Chelsea Room is the polished table damaged by his fist in berating Hitler, together with some lovely chairs and favourite antiques. The walls are hung with pictures by Chelsea artists. All but two are by Whistler's close companion, Walter Greaves. The remaining pair, showing Chelsea Hospital gardens and Chelsea Old Church before wartime bombing, are the work of Ireland's artist friend Hamilton Hay whose tragically early death intervened before his talent could bring him fame. In the long, low Music Room are his two grand pianos, his metronome, the portrait bust of a chorister representing *The Holy Boy,* the Chelsea china smashed by Smokey and restored by Mrs. Kirby, and photographs of Ireland at all ages. In a drawer are wads of letters; the butcher's angry missive which so amused him is as carefully kept as those from famous musicians. His gold medal of the Worshipful Company of Musicians is there together with the hated blackbound notebook in which, as a student, he was ordered to keep account of every penny spent from his guardian's allowance. Only his original manuscripts are missing. Wisely, these have all been lodged in the British Museum for safe keeping.

Even though this was never Ireland's home there is an indefinable aura about it. It is easy to imagine, sitting at his own table with every article and picture around it arranged as at the Mill, that his small, courtly, slightly old-fashioned figure is about to walk through from the music room, with an astringent but unmalicious quip on his lips.

At Gunter Grove it is a very different story. When Ireland left, some twenty-five years ago, he already felt that this was no longer the Chelsea he knew. He would dislike it even more today. At the time of writing, Number 14 is divided into flatlets. The number is roughly chalked on the door and several estate agents' boards stand at the gate. Lorries unceasingly roar past, deafening any musical pilgrim who attempts to stand and stare. As yet London has not honoured the house with a blue plaque.

Today there is a noticeable upsurge of interest in Ireland's compositions. Having chosen him as the subject of their degree theses, students often travel down to Steyning to talk about him with Mrs. Kirby and to feel the atmosphere of his music room. Letters arrive, asking for information about Ireland, from students in New Zealand, Canada, the United States and other foreign countries.

At home, Ireland's best music keeps its place in the permanent concert repertoire, while *Love Unknown* must surely be among the most constantly used of all modern English hymns. *Ireland in C* and *Ireland in F* are sung in cathedrals and greater churches as frequently as the noble Stanford settings.

Converts to Ireland's music are continually being made, as taste begins to react against the dry experimentation of the 1950s and 1960s. Through contact with those who knew him some of these discover the man as well. A story is told of an all-Ireland concert given in Steyning church by performers who had been personal friends. Only the organist was an 'outsider'. At dinner beforehand the 'Ireland Family' became exceedingly merry in exchanging stories of his wit and mimicry, and examples of 'John's little ways'. Next morning the organist telephoned Norah Kirby to say: 'Dr. Ireland must have been a very wonderful man. You were all talking about him with such affection, and bringing him to life.' Such can be the impact of this remarkable personality even at second-hand.

Long ago a choirboy was perceptive enough to sense in Ireland 'a personality that came out and got you'. The same quality is inherent in his music, prompting certain artists to specialise in this composer, such as the pianists Eric Parkin and Alan Rowlands. The latter was still a student at the RCM when he played through much of Ireland's piano music to the composer at Rock Mill. As a result Mr. Rowlands was invited to make many recordings which, because of this close contact, are considered definitive. Curiously, he was not left with the almost inexhaustible store of memories which other visitors took away with them. Instead, it was the indefinable spirit of the place and its owner which stuck in his mind. 'I went through a great deal of his music with him, but I never kept any diary or written record of what happened' Mr.

Rowlands recalled, 'consequently, although my memory of the atmosphere of those visits is quite strong, I am rather short of specific anecdotes . . . as I write I realise that most of my memories are visual.'

Near the beginning of this biography it was suggested that Ireland loved cats almost as much as crotchets. He never forgot, even in old age, all those he had known since boyhood. It seems fitting, therefore, to let Smokey of Rock Mill bring the book to its conclusion.

Night after night after his death the Siamese cried outside his bedroom door. Cats being creatures of habit, she had developed such little rituals as seeming to fetch him downstairs each evening to hear the nine o'clock news; she could not understand why he no longer appeared.

Norah Kirby, made ill by the stress of the past two years, took Smokey and a young Siamese bought to keep her company when she herself went to winter in Cornwall. After the further setback of sustaining a stroke, Mrs. Kirby felt that permanently leaving the Mill and its atmosphere of memories was the right move.

Smokey accepted Steyning as her new home, but she never forgot her master. Every voice associated with him, if heard again, sent her running hopefully towards the music room. One evening, more than nine years later, Smokey jumped up as usual at the first chime of Big Ben. Suddenly she seemed to realise the truth. After standing motionless for a moment she sank to the carpet and lay still.

John Ireland's cat had fetched him for the last time.

12. Gramophone Records available for purchase in 1979

Orchestra		*Publisher*
SRCS.31	A London Overture: Concertino Pastorale; Epic March; The Holy Boy; Minuet and Elegy (A Downland Suite). LONDON PHILHARMONIC ORCHESTRA. SIR ADRIAN BOULT.	Lyrita
RL.25071	Concertino Pastorale BOURNEMOUTH SINFONIETTA. GEORGE HURST.	RCA
SRCS.32	Prelude, The Forgotten Rite; Symphonic Rhapsody, Mai-Dun; Legend for Piano and Orchestra; Overture Satyricon. ERIC PARKIN, LONDON PHILHARMONIC ORCHESTRA. SIR ADRIAN BOULT.	Lyrita
SRCS.36	Concerto for Piano and Orchestra. ERIC PARKIN, LONDON PHILHARMONIC ORCHESTRA. SIR ADRIAN BOULT. (Coupled with 'These Things shall be' – see below.)	Lyrita
SLS.5080	Concerto for Piano and Orchestra. COLIN HORSLEY, ROYAL PHILHARMONIC ORCHESTRA. BASIL CAMERON.	EMI
SRCS.45	Symphonic Prelude, Tritons; Two Symphonic Studies; Suite, The Overlanders; Scherzo and Cortege (Julius Caesar). LONDON PHILHARMONIC ORCHESTRA. SIR ADRIAN BOULT.	Lyrita
ASD.2305	A London Overture (included in 'English Tone Pictures'). LONDON SYMPHONY ORCHESTRA. SIR JOHN BARBIROLLI.	HMV
CHORUS		
SRCS.36	These Things shall be. LONDON PHILHARMONIC CHOIR, JOHN CAROL CASE. LONDON PHILHARMONIC ORCHESTRA. SIR ADRIAN BOULT. (Coupled with Concerto for Pianoforte and Orchestra – see above.)	Lyrita
ZRG.5340	Greater Love hath no Man (included in 'Twentieth Century Church Music'). CHOIR OF St. JOHN'S COLLEGE, CAMBRIDGE. GEORGE GUEST, BRIAN RUNNETT (Organ).	Argo
HQS.1350	Greater Love hath no Man (included in 'Treasury of English Church Music'). CHOIR OF CHICHESTER CATHEDRAL. JOHN BIRCH, RICHARD SEAL (Organ).	HMV

LPB.695	Ex ore innocentium. YORK MINSTER CHOIR. FRANCIS JACKSON.	Abbey
LPB.725	My son is love unknown. NEW COLLEGE CHOIR. DAVID LUMSDEN.	Abbey
LPB.767	My song is love unknown. St. JOHN'S CATHEDRAL CHOIR. WHITEHEAD.	Abbey
LPB.803	Te Deum in F; Adam lay Ybounden; The Holy Boy; New Year Carol; Magnificat and Nunc Dimittis in F; My song is love unknown; Ex ore innocentium; Vexilla Regis; Greater love hath no man. WORCESTER CATHEDRAL CHOIR, WORCESTER FESTIVAL CHORAL SOCIETY, WORCESTER SINFONIA BRASS ENSEMBLE. DONALD HUNT.	Abbey

Brass Band

TWOX.1053	Comedy Overture; A Downland Suite (included in 'Great British Music for Brass'). GUS (Kettering) BAND. GEOFFREY BRAND.	EMI
SXL.6820	Comedy Overture. GRIMETHORPE COLLIERY BAND. ELGAR HOWARTH.	Decca

Chamber Music

SRCS.59	Sextet for horn, clarinet and string quartet; Cello Sonata; Fantasy Sonata for clarinet and piano. MELOS ENSEMBLE, ANDRE NAVARRA (cello), GERVASE DE PEYER (clarinet), ERIC PARKIN (piano).	Lyrita
SRCS.64	Violin Sonata No. 1 in D Minor; Violin Sonata No. 2 in A Minor. YFRAH NEAMAN (violin), ERIC PARKIN (piano).	Lyrita
SAGA.5230	THREE TRIOS for violin, violoncello and pianoforte; Phantasie Trio in A Minor; Trio No. 2 in E (one movement); Trio No. 3 in E (four movements). THE DAVID MARTIN TRIO.	Saga
SAGA.5206	Violin Sonata No. 2 in A Minor; Fantasy Sonata for clarinet and pianoforte; Decorations and The Holy Boy for pianoforte. TESSA ROBBINS (Violin), THEA KING (Clarinet), ALAN ROWLANDS (Pianoforte) (included in 'In Memoriam John Ireland').	Saga
SRCS.98	Phantasie Trio in A Minor; Trio No. 2 in E; Trio No. 3 in E. YFRAH NEAMAN (Violin), JULIAN LLOYD WEBBER (Cello), ERIC PARKIN (Piano).	Lyrita

159

Songs with Piano

ZK.28-9   **THE LAND OF LOST CONTENT**   Argo
The Lent lily; Ladslove; Goal and wicket; The vain
desire; The encounter; Epilogue.

THREE SONGS
Love and friendship; Friendship in misfortune; The
one hope.

THE TRELLIS
(Included in 'Twentieth Century English Songs').
PETER PEARS (Tenor)
BENJAMIN BRITTEN (Pianoforte).

ECS.545   **I HAVE TWELVE OXEN**   Decca
(Included in 'English Songs').
PETER PEARS (Tenor)
BENJAMIN BRITTEN (Pianoforte).

SRCS.65   **SONGS – VOLUME ONE**   Lyrita
Songs of a Wayfarer, Hope the Hornblower; Five Poems
by Thomas Hardy; Three Songs; We'll to the Woods
no more; Marigold; Sea Fever; When Lights go rolling
around the Sky.
BENJAMIN LUXON & ALAN ROWLANDS.

SRCS.66   **SONGS – VOLUME TWO**   Lyrita
Two Songs; Songs Sacred & Profane; Vagabond; Five
XVIth Century Songs; Blow out you Bugles; If there were
Dreams to sell; Spring Sorrow; I have twelve Oxen; The
Bells of San Marie; The Journey; The Merry Month of
May; Santa Chiara; Great Things; If we must part; Tutto
e sciolto; When I am dead my Dearest.
BENJAMIN LUXON & ALAN ROWLANDS.

ASO.2929   The Salley Gardens (included in 'A Pageant of English Song').   HMV
JANET BAKER & GERALD MOORE.

SAGA.5213   Her Song, A Thanksgiving (included in 'An Anthology of   Saga
English Song').
JANET BAKER & MARTIN ISEPP.

GL.25062   The Hills – Partsong   RCA
EXULTATE SINGERS.

DSLO.20   Sea Fever.   L'Oiseau
NORMAN BAILEY acc. G. Parsons.   Lyre

ASD.3545   Sea Fever.   HMV
ROBERT LLOYD.

Piano Solo

RCS.15   London Pieces – Chelsea Reach, Ragamuffin, Soho   Lyrita
Forenoons; Greenways Suite – The Cherry Tree, Cypress,
The Palm and May; Sonatina; Soliloquy; Equinox; On a
Birthday Morning.
ALAN ROWLANDS (Piano).

RCS.23   Sarnia; For Remembrance; Ballade; February's Child; Aubade. Lyrita
ALAN ROWLANDS (Piano).

RCS.24   Piano Sonata; The Towing Path; The Darkened Valley;   Lyrita
Rhapsody; Month's Mind.
ALAN ROWLANDS (Piano).

		Publisher
RCS.28	Decorations – The Island Spell, Moon-glade, The Scarlet Ceremonies; Preludes – The Undertone, Obsession, The Holy Boy, Fire of Spring; In Those Days – Meridian, Daydream; April and Bergomask; Summer Evening; Prelude in E Flat; The Almond Tree. ALAN ROWLANDS (Piano).	Lyrita
RCS.29	Three Pastels – A Grecian Lad, The Boy Bishop, Puck's Birthday; Columbine; Amberley Wild Brooks; Merry Andrew; Sea Idyll; Spring Will Not Wait; Ballade of London Nights. ALAN ROWLANDS (Piano).	Lyrita
SCRS.87	Decorations; Preludes; The Towing Path; London Pieces; Rhapsody; Merry Andrew. ERIC PARKIN.	Lyrita
SRCS.88	Piano Sonata; Summer Evening; April; Amberley Wild Brooks; Soliloquy; On a Birthday Morning; Equinox; Bergomask; The Darkened Valley; For Remembrance. ERIC PARKIN.	Lyrita
SRCS.89	Sonatina; Ballade; February's Child; Aubade; Month's Mind; Green ways; Sarnia. ERIC PARKIN.	Lyrita
SAGA.5445	Aubade (included in 'Recitals, English Music'). RICHARD DEERING.	Saga
SAGA.5206	Decorations, The Holy Boy (included in 'In Memoriam, John Ireland'). ALAN ROWLANDS.	Saga
SDD.444	Sonatina (included in 'English Music'). JOHN McCABE.	Decca
HQS.1414	April; The Almond Tree; Columbine; The Holy Boy; Decorations; Sarnia; Three Dances. DANIEL ADNI.	HMV

*Saga records are available from the Crusade Against All Cruelty to Animals, Humane Education Centre, Avenue Lodge, Bounds Green Road, London N22 4EU.

Lyrita records are expected to be available until at least 1989.

13. John Ireland: List of
Published Works

Chorus and Orchestra

	Date of composition	Publisher
GREATER LOVE HATH NO MAN (Motet)	1912	Stainer & Bell
A Meditation for Passiontide and other seasons,	Orchestrated	
for treble and baritone soli, mixed choir and	1924	
orchestra. (Sometmes called by an alternative		
title 'Many Waters cannot quench Love'.)		
The words selected from the Scriptures		
THESE THINGS SHALL BE	1936–7	Boosey &
Baritone (or tenor) solo, mixed chorus and		Hawkes
orchestra		
Poem from 'A Vista' by John Addington		
Symonds		
VEXILLA REGIS (Op. posth)	1898	Galliard
Hymn for Passion Sunday for mixed chorus,		
brass and organ		
English translation by J. M. Neale from the		
Latin text by Bishop Venantius Fortunatas		
(A.D. 530–609)		

Church Services

EVENING SERVICE in C major	1941	Novello
Mixed choir and organ		
Magnificat		
Nunc Dimittis		
EVENING SERVICE in F major	Published 1915	Novello
Mixed choir and organ		
Magnificat		
Nunc Dimittis		
MORNING SERVICE in C major	1941	Novello
Mixed choir and organ		
Te Deum Laudamus		
Benedictus		
Jubilate Deo		
MORNING SERVICE in F major		Novello
Mixed choir and organ		
Te Deum Laudamus	Published 1907	
Benedictus	Published 1912	
Jubilate Deo	Published 1914	
Benedicite omnia opera	Published 1920	
OFFICE OF THE HOLY COMMUNION in C	1913	Novello
Mixed choir and organ		
PATER NOSTER (The Lord's Prayer)	1913	Novello
from the Office of the Holy Communion in C		
Unaccompanied mixed choir		

	Date of composition	Publisher
NINEFOLD KYRIE in A minor Mixed choir and optional organ For use with the Communion Service in C major	1941	Novello

Hymns

	Date of composition	Publisher
CHRIST THE LORD IS RISEN TODAY (Tune: Sampford) Words by Jane E. Leeson	1948	John Ireland Estate (Copyright owners). (Included in 'Hymns Ancient and Modern' etc.)
GOD OF NATIONS (Tune: Irene) No. 2 of three 'Hymns for the Celebration of Peace' with words by Alfred Moss	1918	Hunter and Longhurst
HOLY FATHER IN THY MERCY (Tune: Eastergate) Words by Isabella S. Stevenson	1905	John Ireland Estate (Copyright owners). Included in 'The English Hymnal' etc.
LORD, KEEP US SAFE (Tune: Vesper Hymn)	Published 1911	John Ireland Estate (Copyright owners).
MIGHTY FATHER, THOU WHOSE AID (Tune: Mighty Father) Based on a hymn by Charles Wesley	1919	John Ireland Estate (Copyright owners). Included in 'The Public School Hymnal' etc.
MY SONG IS LOVE UNKNOWN (Tune: Love Unknown) Words by Samuel Crossman	1919	John Ireland Estate (Copyright owners). Included in 'Songs of Praise' etc.
SING, BROTHERS, SING AND PRAISE YOUR KING (Tune: Chelsea) Words by C. A. Alington	1924	John Ireland Estate (Copyright owners). Included in 'Songs of Praise' etc.
THESE THINGS SHALL BE* (Tune: Fraternity) Words by John Addington Symonds *Except for the words, this hymn has no connection with the work for chorus and orchestra of the same name	Published 1919	Stainer & Bell

Mixed Voice Chorus (S.A.T.B.)	Date of composition	Publisher
ADAM LAY YBOUNDEN (Carol) Unaccompanied Words from a 15th century manuscript	1956	Freeman
CRADLE SONG, A Unaccompanied Poem by William Blake	1912	Stainer & Bell
CUPID Unaccompanied Poem by William Blake	(Early) Published 1961	Galliard
FAIN WOULD I CHANGE THAT NOTE Unaccompanied Poem by Tobias Hume	Published 1921	Novello
GREATER LOVE HATH NO MAN (Motet) A Meditation for Passiontide and other seasons, for treble and baritone soli, mixed choir and organ. (Sometimes called by an alternative title *'Many Waters cannot quench Love'*) The words selected from the Scriptures	1912	Stainer & Bell
HILLS, THE Unaccompanied Poem by James Kirkup Composed for the anthology 'A Garland for the Queen'	1953	Stainer & Bell
HOLY BOY, THE (A Carol of the Nativity) Unaccompanied Poem by Herbert S. Brown An arrangement by the composer of No. 3 of *'Preludes'* for piano	1913 arr. 1941	Boosey & Hawkes
IMMORTALITY Unaccompanied Poem by Henry S. Compton	1942	Boosey & Hawkes
IN PRAISE OF NEPTUNE Unaccompanied Poem by Thomas Campian An arrangement of the unison song of the same title	Published 1911	Ascherberg
MAN IN HIS LABOUR REJOICETH Piano accompaniment Poem by Robert Bridges	1947	Galliard
NEW PRINCE, NEW POMP (Carol) Unaccompanied Poem by Robert Southwell (Sometimes known by he alternative title of *'Behold a simple tender babe'*)	Published 1928	Freeman
NEW YEAR CAROL, A Unaccompanied Poem traditional	1941	Boosey & Hawkes
SPRING, THE SWEET SPRING Unaccompanied Poem by Thomas Nashe	Published 1908	Bosworth
TWILIGHT NIGHT Unaccompanied Poem by Christina Rossetti	1922	Novello
WHEN MAY IS IN HIS PRIME Unaccompanied Poem by Richard Edwardes	1920	Novello

Male Voice Chorus (T.T.B.B. unaccompanied)

	Date of composition	Publisher
ISLAND PRAISE Words from Isaiah	1955	Freeman
THEY TOLD ME, HERACLITUS Poem by William Cory	Published 1924	Boosey & Hawkes

Two-Part Songs with Piano or Organ

AT EARLY DAWN Poem by James Vila Blake (from the German)	Published 1911	Curwen
AUBADE Poem by Sydney Dobell	Published 1912	Novello
ECHOING GREEN, THE Poem by William Blake	1913	Curwen
EVENING SONG Poem by James Vila Blake (from Rückert)	Published 1912	Novello
EX ORE INNOCENTIUM Poem by Bishop W. W. How	1944	Boosey & Hawkes
FULL FATHOM FIVE Poem by Shakespeare	Published 1908	Novello
IN PRAISE OF MAY Poem by Thomas Morley	Published 1909	Novello
IN SUMMER WOODS Poem by James Vila Blake (from the German)	Published 1911	Curwen
MAY FLOWERS Poem by Christina Rossetti	1919	Novello
NEW YEAR CAROL, A Poem traditional	1941	Boosey & Hawkes
SEE HOW THE MORNING SMILES Poem by Thomas Campian	Published 1912	Stainer & Bell
THERE IS A GARDEN IN HER FACE Poem by Richard Alison	Published 1908	Novello

Unison Songs with Piano

ALPINE SONG Poem by James Vila Blake (from the German)	Published 1911	Curwen
BED IN SUMMER Poem by Robert Louis Stevenson	c.1912–13	Curwen
BELL IN THE LEAVES, THE Poem by Eleanor Farjeon	1942	Boosey & Hawkes
BOYS' NAMES Poem by Eleanor Farjeon	1941	Curwen
CHILD'S SONG Poem by Thomas Moore	1913	Ascherberg
FERRY, THE Poem by Christina Rossetti	Published 1921	Novello

	Date of composition	Publisher
FROG AND THE CRAB, THE Poem early 16th century	Published 1909	Ascherberg
GRADUATION SONG (for the University of London) Poem by John Drinkwater	Published 1926	Curwen
IN PRAISE OF NEPTUNE Poem by Thomas Campian	Published 1911	Ascherberg
JOSEPH FELL A-DREAMING Poem by Eleanor Farjeon	1942	Boosey & Hawkes
LOOKING ON Poem by Eleanor Farjeon	Published 1949	Curwen
NEW YEAR CAROL, A Poem traditional	1941	Boosey & Hawkes
O HAPPY LAND Poem by W. J. Linton	1941	Boosey & Hawkes
SEA FEVER Poem by John Masefield	1913	Galliard
SLUMBER SONG Poem by James Vila Blake (from the German)	Published 1933	Novello
SONG OF MARCH, A Poem by James Vila Blake	Published 1918	Novello
SPRING Poem by James Vila Blake (from the German)	Published 1933	Novello
SUNSET PLAY Poem by William Blake	1913	Ascherberg

Solo Songs with Piano or other accompaniments

ADORATION, THE Poem by Arthur Symons	1918	Chester
BED IN SUMMER Poem by Robert Louis Stevenson	c.1912–13	Curwen
BELLS OF SAN MARIE, THE Poem by John Masefield	1919	Galliard
EARTH'S CALL (A Sylvan Rhapsody) Poem by Harold Monro	1918	Dorie
EAST RIDING, THE Poem by Eric Chilman	c.1920	Ashdown
FIVE POEMS BY THOMAS HARDY for baritone voice and piano 1. Beckon to me to come 2. In my sage moments 3. It was what you bore with you, woman 4. The tragedy of that moment 5. Dear, think not that they will forget you	1926	O.U.P.

	Date of composition	Publisher
FIVE XVIth CENTURY POEMS	1938	John Ireland
1. A thanksgiving		Estate
Poem by Bassus		(Copyright
2. All in a garden green		owners)
Poem by Thomas Howell		
3. An aside		
Poem temp. Henry VIII		
4. A report song		
Poem by Nicholas Breton		
5. The Sweet Season		
Poem by Richard Edwardes		
GREAT THINGS	1925	Galliard
Poem by Thomas Hardy		
HAWTHORN TIME	1919	Boosey &
Poem by A. E. Housman		Hawkes
HEART'S DESIRE, THE	c.1917	Boosey &
Poem by A. E. Housman		Hawkes
HOLY BOY, THE	1913	Boosey &
Poem by Herbert S. Brown	arr. 1938	Hawkes
(Arrangement by the composer of No. 3 of		
'Preludes' for pianoforte)		
HOPE THE HORNBLOWER	c.1911	Galliard
Poem by Henry Newbolt		
HYMN TO LIGHT	c.1911	Chappell
Poem by James Vila Blake		
IF THERE WERE DREAMS TO SELL	1918	Boosey &
Poem by Thomas Lovell Beddoes		Hawkes
I HAVE TWELVE OXEN	1918	Boosey &
Poem Early English		Hawkes
J'AI DOUZE BOEUFS	1918	Boosey &
(Edition of 'I Have Twelve Oxen' with		
French text by Lilian Fearn)		
JOURNEY, THE	c.1920	Ashdown
Poem by Ernest Blake		
LAND OF LOST CONTENT, THE	1920–21	Galliard
Six Songs from A. E. Housman's 'A		
Shropshire Lad'		
1. The Lent lily		
2. Ladslove		
3. Goal and wicket		
4. The vain desire		
5. The encounter		
6. Epilogue		
LOVE IS A SICKNESS FULL OF WOES	1921	Boosey &
Poem by Samuel Daniel		Hawkes
MARIGOLD	1913	Doric
1.Youth's spring tribute		
Poem by D. G. Rossetti		
2. Penumbra		
Poem by D. G. Rossetti		
3. Spleen		
Poem by Ernest Dowson, after Verlaine		
MERRY MONTH OF MAY, THE	1921	John Ireland
Poem by Thomas Dekker		Estate
		(Copyright
		owners)

	Date of composition	Publisher
MOTHER AND CHILD (Nursery Rhymes from 'Sing Song') Poems by Christina Rossetti 1. Newborn 2. The only child 3. Hope 4. Skylark and nightingale 5. The blind boy 6. Baby 7. Death parting 8. The garland	1918	John Ireland Estate (Copyright owners)
O HAPPY LAND Poem by W. J. Linton	1941	Boosey & Hawkes
RAT, THE Poem by Arthur Symons	1918	Chester
REMEMBER Poem by Mary Coleridge	1918	John Ireland Estate (Copyright owners)
REST (Repos) Poem by Arthur Symons	1919	Chester
SACRED FLAME, THE Poem by Mary Coleridge	1918	Boosey & Hawkes
SANTA CHIARA (Palm Sunday; Naples) Poem by Arthur Symons	1925	Galliard
SEA FEVER Poem by John Masefield	1913	Galliard
SONG FROM O'ER THE HILL Poem by P. J. O'Reilly	1913	Cramer
SONGS OF A WAYFARER 1. Memory Poem by William Blake 2. When daffodils begin to peer Poem by William Shakespeare 3. English May Poem by D. G. Rossetti 4. I was not sorrowful Poem by Ernest Dowson 5. I will walk on the earth Poem by James Vila Blake	c.1905–11	Boosey & Hawkes
SONGS SACRED AND PROFANE 1. The advent Poem by Alice Meynell 2. Hymn for a child Poem by Sylvia Townsend Warner 3. My fair Poem by Alice Meynell 4. The Salley Gardens Poem by W. B. Yeats 5. The soldier's return Poem by Sylvia Townsend Warner 6. The scapegoat Poem by Sylvia Townsend Warner	1929–31	Schott
SONGS TO POEMS BY THOMAS HARDY 1. Summer schemes 2. Her Song 3. Weathers	1925	Cramer

	Date of composition	Publisher
SPRING SORROW Poem by Rupert Brooke	1918	Boosey & Hawkes
THREE RAVENS, THE (Arranged) Words and melody traditional	c.1920	John Ireland Estate (Copyright owners)

THREE SONGS
1. Love and friendship
  Poem by Emily Bronte
2. Friendship in misfortune
  Poem Anon
3. The one hope
  Poem by D. G. Rossetti
	1926	Galliard

TUTTO E SCIOLTO Poem by James Joyce	c.1932	O.U.P.
TWO SONGS: THE COST **(Songs of a Great War)** Poems by Eric Thirkell Cooper 1. Blind 2. The Cost	1916	Boosey & Hawkes
TWO SONGS Poems by Rupert Brooke 1. The soldier 2. Blow out, you bugles	1917–18	Boosey & Hawkes

TWO SONGS
1. The trellis
  Poem by Aldous Huxley
2. My true love hath my heart
  Poem by Sir Philip Sidney
	1920	Galliard

TWO SONGS
1. Tryst (In Fountain Court)
  Poem by Arthur Symons
2. During music
  Poem by D. G. Rossetti
	1928	O.U.P.

VAGABOND Poem by John Masefield	1922	Galliard
VARIATIONS SUR 'CADET ROUSSELLE' Arrangement of French folk-song, with other arrangements of the same by Bax, Bridge and Goossens French text	c.1920	Chester
WE'LL TO THE WOODS NO MORE Poems by A. E. Housman 1. We'll to the woods no more 2. In boyhood 3. Spring will not wait	1926–27	O.U.P.
WHEN I AM DEAD, MY DEAREST Poem by Christina Rossetti	1924	O.U.P.
WHEN LIGHTS GO ROLLING ROUND THE SKY Poem by James Vila Blake	c.1911	Chappell
YOUR BROTHER HAS A FALCON Poem by Christina Rossetti ('Newborn' the first song of the 'Mother and Child' cycle is published separately under this title)	1918	Boosey & Hawkes

	Date of composition	Publisher
Orchestra		
BAGATELLE	1911 (arr. 1916)	Novello
CONCERTINO PASTORALE For string orchestra 1. Eclogue 2. Threnody 3. Toccata	1939	Boosey & Hawkes
CONCERTO IN E FLAT FOR PIANO AND ORCHESTRA	1930	Chester
EPIC MARCH	1942	Boosey & Hawkes
FORGOTTEN RITE, THE (Prelude)	1913	Galliard
HOLY BOY, THE (Arrangement by the composer of No. 3 of 'Preludes' for piano)	1913 arr. 1941	Boosey & Hawkes
LEGEND FOR PIANO AND ORCHESTRA	1933	Schott
LONDON OVERTURE, A	1936	Boosey & Hawkes
MAI-DUN (Symphonic Rhapsody)	1920–21	Galliard
OVERLANDERS SUITE, THE (op. posth.) Selected and edited from the film score by Charles Mackerras (1965) 1. March: Scorched Earth 2. Romance: Mary and the Sailor 3. Intermezzo: Open Country 4. Scherzo: Brumbies 5. Finale: Night Stampede	1946–47	Boosey & Hawkes
SCORCHED EARTH March from the 'Overlanders' Suite		Boosey & Hawkes
SATYRICON OVERTURE	1946	Galliard
TWO PIECES: MINUET AND ELEGY Freely adapted by the composer from 'A Downland Suite' for brass band. For string orchestra	1933 arr. 1941	Boosey & Hawkes
VARIATIONS ON 'CADET ROUSSELLE' Arrangement of French folk-song (With other arrangements of the same by Bax, Bridge and Goossens) Orchestrated by Eugene Goossens	c.1920 (Orchestrated 1930)	Chester
VILLANELLA (A Miniature) Original for organ Arranged by Ronald Binge	1904 arr. 1949	Ascherberg
Incidental Music		
JULIUS CAESAR Music for the play by Shakespeare	1942	John Ireland Estate (Copyright owners)

170

	Date of composition	Publisher
Brass Band, Military Band, Brass Ensemble		
COMEDY OVERTURE, A For Brass Band	1934	R. Smith
DOWNLAND SUITE, A For Brass Band 1. Prelude 2. Elegy 3. Minuet 4. Round	1933	R. Smith
HOLY BOY, THE (Arrangement for brass ensemble by Robert E. Stepp of No. 3 of 'Preludes' for pianoforte)	1913 arr. 1950	Boosey & Hawkes
MARITIME OVERTURE, A For Military Band (Based on an early unpublished orchestral work)	1944	Boosey & Hawkes

Chamber Music for three or more instruments

HOLY BOY, THE For string quartet (Arrangement by the composer of No. 3 of 'Preludes' for piano)	1913 arr. 1941	Boosey & Hawkes
PHANTASIE TRIO in A minor (in one movement) For Violin, Violoncello and Pianoforte	1908	Galliard
SEXTET For Clarinet, Horn and String Quartet	1898	Galliard
STRING QUARTET No. 1 in D minor (Op. posth.)	1895	Boosey & Hawkes
STRING QUARTET No. 2 in C minor (Op. posth.)	1897	Boosey & Hawkes
TRIO No. 2 in F in one movement For Violin, Violoncello and Pianoforte	1917	Galliard
TRIO No. 3 in F in four movements For Violin, Violoncello and Pianoforte (Rewritten from an unpublished trio of 1913)	1938	Boosey & Hawkes

Violin and Piano

BAGATELLE	1911	Novello
BERCEUSE	1902	Galliard
HOLY BOY, THE (Arrangement by the composer of No. 3 of 'Preludes' for pianoforte)	1913 arr. 1919	Boosey & Hawkes
SONATA No. 1 in D minor	1908–9 (Revised 1917	Galliard
SONATA No. 2 in A minor	1915–17	Boosey & Hawkes

Viola and Piano

	Date of composition	Publisher
SONATA (in G minor) (The viola part arranged from the Sonata for Violoncello and Pianoforte by Lionel Tertis)	1923 arr. 1941	Galliard

Cello and Piano

HOLY BOY, THE (Arrangement by the composer of No. 3 of 'Preludes' for pianoforte)	1913 arr. 1919	Boosey & Hawkes
SONATA (in G minor)	1923	Galliard

Clarinet and Piano

FANTASY SONATA	1943	Boosey & Hawkes

Piano Solo

BALLADE	1929	Schott
BALLADE OF LONDON NIGHTS (Op. posth.)	Published 1968	Boosey & Hawkes
COLUMBINE (Included in 'Down the Centuries', an anthology of piano pieces edited by Leonard Isaacs)	1949 revised 1951	British & Continental
DARKENED VALLEY, THE	1921	Galliard
DECORATIONS 1. The island spell 2. Moon-glade 3. The scarlet ceremonies	1912–13	Galliard
ELEGY Arrangement of movement from 'A Downland Suite' for brass band	1933	Ashdown
EPIC MARCH Arrangement by the composer of the orchestral work	1942	Boosey & Hawkes
EQUINOX	1922	Galliard
GREEN WAYS: Three Lyric Pieces 1. The cherry tree 2. Cypress 3. The palm and may ('The Cherry Tree' is a slightly revised version of 'Indian Summer', originally published in a Danish music journal in 1932)	1937	Freeman
IN THOSE DAYS: Two Pieces 1. The Daydream 2. Meridian	1895	Schott

	Date of composition	Publisher
LEAVES FROM A CHILD'S SKETCHBOOK 1. By the mere 2. In the meadow 3. The hunt's up	1918	Galliard
LONDON PIECES 1. Chelsea Reach 2. Ragamuffin 3. Soho forenoons	1917–20	Galliard
MINUET Arrangement of movement from 'A Downland Suite' for brass band	1933	Ashdown
MERRY ANDREW	1918	Ascherberg
MONTH'S MIND	1933	Galliard
ON A BIRTHDAY MORNING	1922	Galliard
PRELUDE in E flat major	1924	Galliard
PRELUDES 1. The undertone 2. Obsession 3. The Holy Boy (A Carol of the Nativity) 4. Fire of spring	1913–15	Boosey & Hawkes
RHAPSODY	1915	Boosey & Hawkes
RONDO (Separate edition of finale from Sonatina)	1926–27	OIU.P.
SARNIA: An Island Sequence 1. Le Catioroc 2. In a May morning 3. Song of the springtides	1940–41	Boosey & Hawkes
SEA IDYLL, A	1900	Chester
SOLILOQUY	1922	Galliard
SONATA (in E minor-major)	1918–20	Galliard
SONATINA	1926–27	O.U.P.
SPRING WILL NOT WAIT (Final item of the song-cycle 'We'll to the woods no more')	1927	O.U.P.
SUMMER EVENING	1919	Ascherberg
THREE PASTELS 1. A Grecian lad (Rewritten from an early MS) 2. The boy bishop 3. Puck's birthday	1941	Galliard
THREE DANCES (Original title 'Three Rustic Dances') 1. Gipsy dance 2. Country dance 3. Reapers' dance	1913	Curwen
TOWING PATH, THE	1918	Galliard
TWO PIECES 1. For remembrance 2. Amberley Wild Brooks	1921	Galliard

	Date of composition	Publisher
TWO PIECES 1. April 2. Bergomask	1924–5	Galliard
TWO PIECES 1. February's child 2. Aubade	1929–30	Schott
VILLANELLA (A Miniature) (The composer's free arrangement of the organ piece)	1912 arr. 1950	Ascherberg

Organ

ALLA MARCIA	1911	Novello
CAPRICCIO	1911	Stainer & Bell
ELEGIAC ROMANCE	1902 revised 1958	Novello
ELEGY (Arrangement by Alec Rowley of a movement from 'A Downland Suite' for brass band)	1923 arr. 1940	Ashdown
HOLY BOY, THE (Arrangement by Alec Rowley of No. 3 of 'Preludes' for piano)	1913 arr. 1919	Boosey & Hawkes
MEDITATION ON JOHN KEBLE'S ROGATIONTIDE HYMN	1958	Freeman
MINIATURE SUITE Compiled from revised versions of: 1. Intrada 2. Villanella 3. Menuetto Impromptu	1912 revised 1944	Ascherberg
SURSUM CORDA	1911	Novello

Transcriptions of other composers

MEINE SEELE ERHEBT DEN HERREN (My Soul doth magnify the Lord) Chorale Prelude by J. S. Bach, arranged for pianoforte (Included in 'A Bach Book for Harriet Cohen')	1932	O.U.P.
CONCERTO IN G minor for Viola and Orchestra by Cecil Forsyth, arranged published 1904 for viola and pianoforte	Published 1904	Schott

Bibliography

Bacharach, A. L.	British Music of our Time (includes article on Ireland by Ralph Hill)
Kirby, Norah	John Ireland: Catalogue of Works (with Foreword by Sir Adrian Boult)
Longmire, John	John Ireland: Portrait of a Friend (John Baker)
Schafer, Murray	British Composers in Interview (Faber) (includes interview with Ireland)
Scott, Stuart	The Chamber Music of John Ireland (Produced by Stuart Scott supported by North West Arts Assn.)
Tydeman, R.	Without a City Wall: Guide to the Church of the Holy Sepulchre and the Musicians' Chapel
—	Dictionary of National Biography — entry on John Ireland by Julian Herbage (in preparation)

Musical Index

177

General Index

179

180

181